*freeing from being a
prisoner of the past*

*Jim Hunt
march 92*

AAMAC

Adults
Anonymous
Molested
As Children

BOB U.

CompCare Publishers

2415 Annapolis Lane
Minneapolis, Minnesota 55441

U., Bob, 1943–
    Adults Anonymous Molested as Children: a twelve-step program for
healing and recovery / Bob U.
        p. cm.
        ISBN 0-89638-240-0
1. Adult child sexual abuse victims—Mental health. 2. Adult child sexual abuse
victims—Rehabilitation. 3. Adults Anonymous Molested as Children. I. Title.
RC569.5.A28U15 1991
616.85'83—dc20   91-1989

Cover by Jeremy Gale   •
Interior design by MacLean & Tuminelly

Inquiries, orders, and catalog requests should be addressed to:
CompCare Publishers
2415 Annapolis Lane
Minneapolis, Minnesota 55441
Call toll free 800/328-3330
Minnesota residents 612/559-4800

To all adults molested as children who wish to exercise their courage to heal and participate in their own recovery; who value free and open availability of recovery for AMACs, regardless of their past; and who believe that anonymity and privacy are their natural right as human beings—this book and program are dedicated.

CONTENTS

PART ONE: BASIC TEXT

PART TWO: PERSONAL EXPERIENCES

PART THREE: THE AAMAC ORGANIZATION

FOREWORD

It all began with one man's promise to a total stranger: "Someday all AMACs will have a place to go for help where there will be no questions asked; no intake procedures or prescreening; no dues or fees and very few rules." This book is the first step in fulfilling that promise made by Bob U., our founder and primary author, to an AMAC as she ran out of his office in panic and fear because of the questionnaire she would have to fill out if she wanted help from the agency that employed him. She never heard his promise, but he kept it anyway. Shortly thereafter, Bob held a meeting with a small group of AMACs whom he was helping. His idea was to start a meeting closed to all but AMACs, so that people who did not want to participate in other kinds of treatment, who valued their natural right to anonymity and privacy, could get help. It would be fashioned after other anonymous programs, but not cloned. This founder felt that AMACs needed and deserved a special type of recovery, and the die was cast. The first AAMAC workshop met soon afterward, in June of 1986, and has continued ever since.

These first workshops were open-ended. In other words, crosstalk was allowed, but the confrontations often got out of hand. Although a great deal of healing resulted, after the initial catharsis, confrontation obstructed further healing and recovery. One by one, members drifted away from the workshops. Many simply moved out of the area and never organized AAMAC workshops in their new locations.

Through voluntary group-conscience, following Bob's suggestions and guidance, the workshops changed over to the traditional anonymous program format ruling out crosstalk and began using an adapted Twelve Steps in their ongoing recovery. After five drafts, our book is now ready for publication. There will be a second edition once the voice of AAMAC, the General Service Conference, is activated sometime in the summer of 1993 or 1994, when the program has settled nationally and adequate healing recovery has occurred among its members.

We have developed several books, booklets, and pamphlets specifically for AAMAC. The Program has proven itself beyond any doubt to be effective as an ongoing tool in the recovery and maintenance of

AMACs. The Program works. AAMAC states that it can be some things to all AMACs, but that it cannot be all things to all AMACs. We strongly urge our members to seek psychotherapy with qualified professionals who are able to treat them as AMACs.

From Victorville, California, to the entire nation is quite a step in reaching out to AMACs who still suffer. There is much to do, and our AAMAC World Services Office, Inc. is certain to be overworked and underfunded for some time. Once your workshop is started, please wait ninety days before registering it with AAMAC WSO, Inc. Be patient awaiting a response. We are self-supporting through our own contributions. Once your workshops begin accumulating funds, and if you wish to contribute financially to your Program, make your checks or money orders out to AAMAC, and mail them to AAMAC WSO, Inc., P.O. Box 662, Apple Valley, CA 92307. As soon as we have ample funding, we will print pamphlets and booklets, along with other books to help us in our recovery and maintenance. Be sure to register your workshop so we can send you notices when new publications are available. Unlike our main text, they will not be available in bookstores.

We look forward to lasting healing and recovery together in Adults Anonymous Molested As Children.

Sincerely,
AAMAC WSO, Inc.

PREFACE

AAMAC literature has been approved by a consensus of adults who were molested as children, members of the AAMAC program, professional therapists, and private non-AMAC citizens. We claim no authority on any subject except our own experience. Our primary purpose in publishing our literature is to recover ourselves and to help other AMACs who are still suffering. Our literature is meant only to suggest structure and approaches to problems: since we are the people who have suffered from our molestation as children, we have something to say about the matter.

Personal experiences contained in this book are candid and explicit in nature. We accept no responsibility should any reader feel offended. We want to share the truth about what happened and how we live now. In our attempt to eliminate sexism from our literature, we have alternated the usage of "he" and "she."

Our book entitled *ADULTS ANONYMOUS MOLESTED AS CHILDREN* is an introduction to our Program. It provides a guide for starting AAMAC workshops, offers general information, and serves as the main text for our Bookstudy workshops. Our Twelve Steps and Twelve Traditions were adapted and modified from those of Alcoholics Anonymous. Although our programs are not affiliated except in a spirit of cooperation, we are grateful that AA was there to pave the way as an example for other anonymous programs to follow.

ACKNOWLEDGMENTS

Many people have participated in the development of our book. We especially acknowledge those first members of Adults Anonymous Molested As Children who contributed their personal experiences, which will forever remain part of our literature. Your courage to heal, to tell the truth about yourselves, is a great inspiration for other AMACs seeking recovery. We are grateful to the AMACs in our society who have worked so hard and stayed with us over the years to help us become a national society of AMACs, by AMACs, for AMACs; what goes around comes around. We also appreciate the aid of the AMACs, professionals, and private citizens who helped develop the consensus expressed in this book.

We thank C. H. Patterson, Ph.D., for his support of our movement. The hours Ralph Hines gave us, printing the first drafts of our literature, provided us with materials to study. Ralph was an important factor in our getting started, and he helped us carry the message to AMACs who still suffer. CompCare Publishers has given us warm and caring patience, and has respected our Traditions.

Finally, I thank the many people who provided me with nurturance or personal assistance during the writing: Kathy, Paulene, Cristi, Clayton, Ralph, Carolyn, Randy, Janice, Dave, Joan, Crissy, Irene, Marv, Holly, Bob, Carl, John, and Mac, just to mention a few.

These and all the other people who have encouraged the establishment of AAMAC and the publication of this book have our profound gratitude.

In love, unity, and service,
Bob U.

A PROFESSIONAL'S OPINION

Whether sexual child abuse has increased, or whether it has been increasingly recognized and brought to light, is not clear. But it is clear that it constitutes a significant social and psychological problem with continuing effects on the lives of its victims. These victims often, if not usually, feel alone, isolated, and different; they suffer in their own silent worlds. As adults they seldom seek psychotherapy, either unaware of the source of their unhappiness or skeptical of finding understanding help from a professional psychotherapist. Affiliation with others in a group offers escape from isolation into a community of those who share a significant common experience cutting across differences in race, creed, color, sex, or social status. That this is a powerful experience leading to change and even healing is demonstrated by other such self-help groups.

Adults Anonymous Molested As Children (AAMAC) is not a professional group or society, and makes no claims as such. It is not engaged in providing psychotherapy. But the experience of participating in an AAMAC workshop can be highly therapeutic. The principles and procedures enunciated are sound and in agreement with the essence of good psychotherapy. The avoidance of pressure or demand for personal disclosure creates a nonthreatening, accepting, understanding atmosphere. It is only in such an atmosphere that helpful self-disclosure occurs. There is no guarantee that the group meeting will lead to recovery or cure; it may or may not. Participants whose problems have snowballed or may be related to other sources than molestation may need additional professional therapy. But the group experience cannot but be helpful to the vast majority of sincere, motivated participants. AAMAC represents a movement whose time has come. It will certainly meet with success if it keeps to the purposes and principles outlined in this book.

C. H. Patterson, Ph.D.
University of South Carolina, Greensboro
January 1987

THE TWELVE STEPS OF ALCOHOLICS ANONYMOUS

1. We admitted we were powerless over alcohol—that our lives had become unmanageable.
2. Came to believe that a Power greater than ourselves could restore us to sanity.
3. Made a decision to turn our will and our lives over to the care of God, as we understood Him.
4. Made a searching and fearless moral inventory of ourselves.
5. Admitted to God, to ourselves, and to another human being the exact nature of our wrongs.
6. Were entirely ready to have God remove all these defects of character.
7. Humbly asked Him to remove our shortcomings.
8. Made a list of all persons we had harmed, and became willing to make amends to them all.
9. Made direct amends to such people wherever possible, except when to do so would injure them or others.
10. Continued to take personal inventory and when we were wrong, promptly admitted it.
11. Sought through prayer and meditation to improve our conscious contact with God, as we understood Him, praying only for knowledge of His will for us and the power to carry that out.
12. Having had a spiritual awakening as the result of these steps, we tried to carry this message to alcoholics, and to practice these principles in all our affairs.

THE TWELVE TRADITIONS OF ALCOHOLICS ANONYMOUS

1. Our common welfare should come first; personal recovery depends upon AA unity.
2. For our group purpose there is but one ultimate authority—a loving God as He may express Himself in our group conscience. Our leaders are but trusted servants; they do not govern.
3. The only requirement for AA membership is a desire to stop drinking.
4. Each group should be autonomous except in matters affecting other groups or AA as a whole.
5. Each group has but one primary purpose—to carry its message to the alcoholic who still suffers.
6. An AA group ought never endorse, finance, or lend the AA name to any related facility or outside enterprise, lest problems of money, property, and prestige divert us from our primary purpose.
7. Every AA group ought to be fully self-supporting, declining outside contributions.
8. Alcoholics Anonymous should remain forever nonprofessional, but our service centers may employ special workers.
9. AA, as such, ought never be organized; but we may create service boards or committees directly responsible to those they serve.
10. Alcoholics Anonymous has no opinion on outside issues; hence the AA name ought never be drawn into public controversy.
11. Our public relations policy is based on attraction rather than promotion; we need always maintain personal anonymity at the level of press, radio, and films.
12. Anonymity is the spiritual foundation of all our traditions, ever reminding us to place principles before personalities.

AAMAC TWELVE STEPS

Our AAMAC Twelve Steps are meant only as suggestions. The term "a power greater than ourselves" is a general term for God, the group, truth, therapy, or whatever we may know the power to be.

1. We admitted that we were powerless over having been molested as children and that parts of our lives had become unmanageable.
2. Came to believe that a power greater than ourselves could help restore us to sanity.
3. Made a decision to share our will and our lives with a power greater than ourselves, keeping an open mind and accepting direction from those who are helping us.
4. Made a searching and fearless moral inventory of ourselves.
5. Admitted to ourselves and to another person the exact nature of our problems.
6. Were entirely ready to accept the help we need to reduce our shortcomings and defects of character.
7. Humbly asked a power greater than ourselves to continue helping us in our recovery by giving us strength to work on our problems.
8. Made a list of all persons we had harmed and became willing to make amends to them.
9. Made direct amends to such people wherever possible, except when to do so would injure them or others.
10. Continued to take personal inventory and, when we were wrong, promptly admitted it.
11. Sought through prayer or meditation to improve our conscious-contact with a power greater than ourselves, expecting only knowledge, direction, and the courage to heal.
12. Having improved as a result of working these Steps, we tried to carry this message to others who were molested as children, and to practice these principles in all of our affairs.

None among us has been able to maintain anything like perfect adherence to these principles. We are not saints. The point is that we are willing to improve. These Steps are guides to progress. We claim progress rather than perfection. Those of us who practice these Steps find that we have stronger purpose for recovery.

AAMAC TWELVE TRADITIONS

1. Our common welfare must come first. Personal recovery depends upon AAMAC unity.
2. For our purpose there is but one authority: a loving power greater than ourselves as expressed in our group conscience. Our leaders are but trusted servants. They do not govern.
3. The only requirements for membership are an age of eighteen or more and a desire to recover from having been molested as a child.
4. Each workshop should be autonomous except in matters affecting other workshops or AAMAC as a whole.
5. Each workshop has the purpose to help ourselves recover and to carry our message to AMACs who still suffer.
6. An AAMAC workshop ought never to endorse, finance or lend the AAMAC name to any related facility or outside enterprise lest problems of money, property and prestige divert us from our primary purpose.
7. Every workshop ought to be self-supporting, declining outside contributions.
8. Adults Anonymous Molested As Children should remain forever non-professional, but our service centers may employ special workers.
9. AAMAC, as such, ought never to be organized, but we may create service boards directly responsible to those they serve.
10. AAMAC has no opinions on outside issues; hence our name ought never to be brought into public controversy.
11. Our public relations policy is based on attraction rather than promotion; we must always maintain the anonymity of other members. Our personal anonymity is a matter of choice so long as we are not speaking for AAMAC as a whole. If we cannot speak well of other members, then we should not speak of them at all.
12. Anonymity is the spiritual foundation of all our traditions, ever reminding us to place principles before personalities.

1

BASIC TEXT

1

WE HAVE BEGUN

But, where do I begin? Begin at the beginning.
But, where is the beginning? The beginning is
now. You are here, the time is now, therefore
you have begun.

We adults who were molested as children are truly yesterday's children, lost in adulthood for many years. Our past traumas were sealed within us to corrupt our future, and we could find no escape other than the self-destructive paths we followed as imitation adults. Who would listen to us? Who would guide us? Who would fill the voids of our childhood? We grew up feeling abandoned, guilty, and betrayed.

NOW OUR TIME HAS COME! We want to banish the fear that haunts us, and the phantoms of anger and resentment that have dominated our thoughts. We want to conquer our mistaken sense of guilt and our feelings of betrayal, abandonment, and mistrust, replacing them with pride in ourselves as people. We grew up with self-destructive feelings because we had no other option: they helped us to survive. Now we take joy in the knowledge that we can change the way we think about ourselves and our traumatic past. The people who violated our innocence and ended our childhood may no longer live in our minds rent-free. We are fortunate survivors, searchers, and truthseekers who wish to turn away from dark secrets and hidden agendas and come out of our agony into the light of recovery.

Our program exists not only for self-help and mutual support, although these are some of our primary functions. We share our experience as men and women who were molested in childhood, finding strength and hope in our Five Legacies of Recovery and Service, our AAMAC Twelve Steps, and our Twelve Traditions. But we are also a publishing and writing society of AMACs, by AMACs, and for AMACs, intent upon carrying our message of hope in books and pamphlets to those who still suffer alone. We know their feelings of frustration and hopelessness. We share their experience. We intend to become a world society, to help people of every nationality to rise above the personal stigma of their childhood experience. Our lives have proven that we can recover from seeming hopelessness. Accounts of our experiences will help others understand AMACs as they help AMACs understand themselves.

Most of us were reluctant to admit that we had been molested as children, feeling that anyone who knew about our past would reject us. Especially embarrassing is the fact that many of us were molested by perpetrators of the same sex. Many researchers think that as many males are molested in childhood as females. Yet fewer males than females seek help and are identified as victims of childhood sexual abuse. The reason, we suspect, is our country's misunderstanding of healthy masculinity. For all of us, male and female, our experiences are abhorrent, yet they sometimes felt good, so we developed pleasure conflicts as a result. We grew up uncertain of our masculine or feminine identity. In AAMAC, we are not judged guilty for our childhood experiences or for the feelings and attitudes that have tainted our adult lives.

Our condition as AMACs is not a disease or illness. Although many of us suffer from one or more related problems such as alcoholism, drug addiction, or emotional disorders, these are only symptoms of our underlying problem. Our affliction is hopeless entrapment in our childhood memories and traumas. Those secrets must be brought to light if we are to recover. Being treated for other problems will not heal our affliction. Treatment for depression or alcoholism that does not deal specifically with our childhood abuse will not help us for long. Unless the abuse is faced squarely, dealt with directly, and firmly accepted, any progress will usually be painfully slow and not very fruitful. We know this only because we have been there.

Childhood sexual abuse annihilates happiness. The emotional baggage AMACs carry into adulthood results in sad spouses and parents; disrupted families; disoriented lives of blameless children; inappropriate suspicion and feelings of betrayal when none occurred; insecurity; horrendous guilt; disgusted and frustrated friends; fierce resentment; under- and over-compensation; pleasure conflicts; anger-rage-hate cycles; personalities that shift between a need to be cared for and a need to not be cared for. Just to mention some of the related disorders we suffer from.

Anyone could add to the list. It is no wonder that uninformed people say things that hurt us. "I don't have a problem with my life, so why should you?" they say. "She's just no good!" "For crying out loud, why don't you just quit screwing up?" "If you are having so many problems, why the hell don't you get some help?" "He could do better if he really wanted to." "More problems, huh? I'm not surprised." "You don't need those stupid programs. They're for weaklings." Uncomprehending observers of our lives often sum up their disapproval with a standard question: "Look, we all had problems growing up. What the hell makes you think that you had it any worse than the rest of us?"

Most people do not yet understand what our experiences have done to us, but that is no excuse for us to remain dysfunctional. Others have no frame of reference that allows them to reach alternate conclusions. Hidden disabilities are hard to recognize and measure. A person suffering from the loss of a limb is visibly disadvantaged, compared to someone with intact arms and legs. But the handicap of a person who had a chunk of his life ripped out of him is not apparent. Even we AMACs lack knowledge about ourselves; we feel more frustrated and critical about our own failures than our acquaintances do. We cannot view our disability objectively; we can only feel it. With practice in recovery, we begin to see more clearly; as we meet and learn to love people like ourselves, we begin to understand what we do that frustrates our friends and families.

Recognizing our nature opens our minds, where the molested child still lives and suffers, unrecognized by anyone, including ourselves. Childhood sexual abuse is never forgotten. If our minds block the traumas of our childhood, our bodies remember. Odors, touches, tinglings, posture, and the combinations of gestures we call body language all trigger those memories. We can grow more conscious of these triggers by listening to each other in our workshops.

Through sharing experience, strength, and hope, we have discovered that our symptoms often occur in clusters of two or more. One symptom or more may be diagnosed as the cause for the others when, in fact, the whole cluster results from our hidden childhood history. In some of us, these symptoms have always been evident. Others, however, enter adult life as reasonable, moderate people. We get married and begin to settle into adult life, and suddenly problems begin. A spouse gets caught molesting a child. The AMAC begins molesting a child after an ongoing dysfunctional relationship. Unexplained insecurities arise. Sudden onsets of intense sexual fantasies override normal sex life. Without warning, feelings of mistrust, betrayal, and jealousy increase or recur. Frigidity, impotence, or bisexual attractions mar relationships. Discomfort in the presence of the opposite sex, or the same sex, or discomfort from feeling discomfort makes our social life uneasy. Radical personality changes and emotional fluctuations come and go abruptly. Migraine headaches incapacitate some of us. Feelings of extreme guilt and sadness, fears of discovery, self-loathing, and low self-esteem flash in quick succession or last for days.

Most AMACs are familiar with hot-and-cold-running emotions, anger-rage-hate cycles, conflicting affection and distrust of society, feelings of loneliness, and a sense of estrangement from themselves and the human race. Even in the face of such anguish, however, we are not helpless. In AAMAC, we can band together with others like ourselves. Our AAMAC society helps us to understand the continuing effects of our childhood experience and to find a place in the mainstream of life. Our own happiness and peace of mind depend in part upon helping others.

When we admitted that we had been molested as children, we determined to do something about that and accept responsibility for our adult lives. We realized that, if we are to keep what we have learned, we have to give it away. Once we began meeting together, we did not become bleeding hearts. We do not feel sorry for one another. We rolled up our sleeves and went to work on ourselves. That is why we call our meetings "workshops." We are very busy working on ourselves by talking about things we never thought we could share with another human being.

As the personal experiences in this book reflect, in AAMAC, we become quite candid about what happened to us as kids, but our openness is a matter of personal choice. Members of our society reveal only what they want to talk about voluntarily. After attending a few of our workshops, many of us have found that revelation is actually a healing relief. Some accounts are more candid and detailed than others, but we all participate in the healing from others' sharing. Here, among our own, we can speak freely about anything we choose. That is why, when an AMAC tells his story, the workshop stops to listen for an unlimited time.

All AMACs have their own hell to go through. We understand this problem, and we know how to deal with it. In AAMAC, we participate equally in life, discovery, and recovery. We insist that all of our workshops be open to both men and women, never limiting our groups to either gender. There is a great deal for each of us to learn about people of the opposite sex, and about the similarities in our feelings and fears, our needs and wants. People who are not ready for mixed groups are not ready for Adults Anonymous Molested As Children.

Because of the sexually explicit content and sensitivity of our workshop discussions, we do not allow non-AMACs or children to be present; indeed, allowing a child to be present would constitute another form of molestation. That is why our workshops admit only AMACs and people exploring whether they are AMACs. We make no exception to our requirement that participants must be eighteen years of age or more.

Many AMACs doubt that they are in our class. They suffer from a belief that they are different: they can straighten out their trouble-ridden lives by themselves. The doubters think that all their past experiences in living, coupled with some shallow knowledge about themselves from reading a self-help book or two, enable them to handle life. Although we wish them the best of everything, such vain attempts sadden us, for we know that one is a lonely number. We too have thought these same thoughts countless times, and have been disappointed. After even intense psychotherapy, most of us relapsed back into our old behavior. We did not have a long-term maintenance program to help us follow through on our living problems and to discover alternate solutions. We forgot our addiction to old attitudes, emotions, and behaviors. And addiction is not too strong a term. How could we have wandered into the same pitfalls repeatedly unless we were blindly addicted to dysfunctional behavior and emotions, ruled by our obsessions, lost in the depths of our secrets, and sealed in sadness? It takes time and self-searching honesty, along with companionable support for change over the long haul of a lifetime. We have learned the hard way. We hope that others will accept AAMAC's help before they suffer so far along the solitary road.

AMACs can be found among all groups in any society. They are among the people exhibiting every kind of problem: suicide, substance abuse, crime, divorce, domestic violence, anorexia, multiple personality disorders, food addiction, mental illness of all kinds, sexual dysfunctions of every character or combination, and behavioral problems of every conceivable nature. Most AMACs suffer from not just one, but several types of problems. Awareness of our great numbers slowly increases as we turn up in treatment programs for child abuse, codependency, domestic violence, emotional illness, drug and alcohol abuse, and Twelve Step programs of every kind. Those who are recovering from AMACism, the syndrome of effects from childhood molestation, must carry the hope of recovery to those who still suffer.

Some AMACs who come through our doors do not have good intentions for themselves or, unfortunately, for us. They feel abandoned and betrayed; anger and mistrust plague them. They are searching for something, but are unsure exactly what it is. Others have come to complain about life in general, but have no intention of changing themselves in order to improve their situation. Some come to save marriages or to seek revenge on the ghosts of their dysfunctional past. Still others want to get the system off their backs. At this early stage, many resist the program. All of these behaviors are symptoms.

Many of the people who come to our workshops for the first time feel hopeless. They may be facing bleak futures. They may be in the remote depths of depression, isolated from themselves and the world at large. They are full of lifelong despair. These new members of AAMAC carry in with them many related problems which may not seem to be related to their childhood abuse. They may feel defenseless against society and the rough realities born of our self-seeking, abrasive world.

These AMACs are at their lowest ebb. The stark and ugly facts are that, in addition to their being AMACs themselves, a few of them may also be perpetrators. We must keep uppermost in our minds that an AMAC is an AMAC, first, last, and always. All else is but symptoms. We are a support group, not an attack group. We can love the person while hating what she has done. By separating the transgressor from her transgressions, we do ourselves a kindness. These AMAC perpetrators afford us the opportunity to rid ourselves of our haunting past through acts of love. That is the true healing process. Above all else, we are not here to hate those who molested us as children, or their surrogates. We can turn over our pain to its rightful owner and rid ourselves of the burden and guilt for all of the crimes against us.

We welcome all AMACs. Their many ways of resisting change only indicate the severity of their need. We are straightforward, however, in our refusal to permit disruption of our recovery. Those who stay dedicate themselves to recovery, choosing not to carry their pain through life. We do not come to AAMAC to die. We come here to heal and learn that life can be worthwhile. We work hard, and we get the job done!

Most AMACs do not understand why they lead troubled lives. Many prefer to go untreated, fearing what might happen. They may have been misdiagnosed by uninformed therapists. They may have had no follow-up after psychotherapy that seemed successful. We have all experienced horrible relapses into hopelessness, but now we have an effective maintenance program. We are proud of what we stand for as individuals and as a society of AMACs helping AMACs. We have achieved together what we could never accomplish alone. We claim progress rather than perfection.

Anonymity at our workshops is our promise of privacy to everyone. Protecting one another's identity is essential to our unity and survival. Confidentiality is also crucial. Though we are not a secret society, we think it wise to maintain a low profile and not to reveal our personal lives indiscriminately. Membership does not qualify us to conduct AAMAC business without authorization, especially in the press, on radio or TV, or in other public ways. We are careful to elect our representatives wisely and check out questions with AAMAC World Services Office before stepping into unfamiliar territory. We neither endorse nor oppose any causes, and we do not become involved in public controversy.

Showing our faces publicly is a matter of individual decision. Some of us may be asked to speak in the media, but AMACs need not do so unless they choose. Of course, the issue of attraction rather than promotion comes in here. Some may consider this publicity to be promotion, but so long as we present ourselves in good taste, the exposure is a means of informing other AMACs that help is available. There is a fine line here, but we must at least acquaint the public with our existence. We use the information media only to reach a greater number of AMACs than we otherwise could.

Even after our initial recovery, we AMACs must continuously adjust our attitudes, emotions, and behavior to new realities in a constructive way. As long as we can find a place to meet together, we should continue to gather. We place our AAMAC workshop schedules in local newspapers for that reason.

We use no professional therapists. We charge no dues or fees, relying instead upon members' contributions, time, and talents. The time to serve will come for each of us. Recovery is our main priority, however, and we do not expect human sacrifice beyond a comfortable and constructive giving. For us, an act of service is an act of love rather than a profession. Much work remains in the establishment of our AAMAC society. Our program is growing, and we are learning as we grow. Though change is healthy, we try to change with caution. We hope that AMACs who read our literature will be inspired to pioneer new AAMAC workshops in their own areas. Chapter 17, "Workshop Information and Guidelines," will help. Individuals and workshops may also write AAMAC WSO, Inc. for advice. The key to our survival is our accessibility to other AMACs. When enough workshops are established, we will print directories listing those which are registered, so be sure to inform us of yours. Simply write for the necessary forms.

We do not claim that our literature is the final word on anything. Nor is it the word of experts and professionals. We only mean to suggest a way of life and thought. The actions any reader bases on our literature are his own choice and responsibility. We like to hear from readers; should you have something to say, pro or con, please write to us and let us know your thoughts as your contribution to future materials and editions of this book.

We urge our members to seek private psychotherapy initially in conjunction with committed work in AAMAC. Even though we all share variations of the same problems, we can't address them, for ourselves or for each other, as a qualified therapist does. A therapist can formulate an overall game plan. Our secrets must be brought out into the sunlight of the workshops, but our symptoms must also be identified clearly and treated. Through our own experiences, we have learned the necessity of checking out a therapist before beginning treatment. Ask some questions; assure yourself that the therapist is qualified to treat adults who were sexually abused as children. You hire a therapist's services; she is not doing you a favor, but earning a living. Therapists for AMACs must be able to focus on the root causes of the life problems which are merely the symptoms of childhood trauma.

Before, during, and after psychotherapy, AAMAC keeps us abreast of our changes and comforts us. Our answers are living answers to living problems, and they change as we change. With the combination of professionals and peers, we can outgrow our dysfunctions and learn to live reasonably happy and productive lives. In AAMAC, we can band together with others like ourselves. Our AAMAC society helps us to repair our adult lives and find a place. Our own happiness and peace of mind depend in part upon our helping others.

2

THE HEART OF THE MATTER

If any should ask how much we love one
another, let our answer be, enough to tell the
truth about ourselves.

What was it that we didn't want to see about ourselves? Many of us still don't know for sure. Some of us have concluded that we feared knowing in general. We feared the discovery, by ourselves and others, of our true identity. Fear and shame are the twin bases of all our trouble.

Most of us really thought that we were bad people and felt guilty all our lives, as if we were ourselves to blame for others' acts. This is a classic AMAC symptom. We feared the bad person we thought we would find buried deep within ourselves. In effect, the perpetrators were living in our minds, and we thought that they somehow were ourselves. We took their responsibility, as if it were we who had seduced them. Social and religious attitudes about morality also magnified our childhood sexual experiences. It never occurred to us that we had not initiated the acts done to us! We didn't know any better, but only did as authority figures directed or enticed us to do. We are not bad! How can helpless children, manipulated by clever adults, be held responsible and accountable for such things? Once we took an honest look at these facts, we began to realize where our feelings of self-loathing came from, a significant discovery for most of us.

When we were children, we thought only with our feelings. Not until our minds began to mature did we learn to cover our feelings with sophisticated thoughts which we now know were forms of denial. We grew up with those guilt-ridden thoughts and became addicted to them as adults. We began to bury our past under excuses, blind justifications, and blame, along with acquired feelings of guilt and shame. As adults, we can choose to think more clearly. Mental blocks may cause us to resist changing what we can. That is why an AMAC's denial runs so deep.

There's a good chance that we owe some apologies along our way into adulthood. Before we recovered, most of us drifted through other people's lives, leaving a trail of pain. We had become destructive in one way or another. Certain that no one who knew the truth about us could accept us, we masked our real selves. We swung from one extreme to another, time after painful time, looking for matching personalities so we could fit in with other people. We judged our insides by other people's outsides. With distorted perception, we paid close attention to the worst in everyone and everything and saw positive attributes only fleetingly. Thinking that we were bad, we acted bad and expected others to do the same. The depth of our self-deception, we have learned in our recovery, is astonishing. No one defended us as children; we defended ourselves to compensate. Our very dysfunctions are survival strategies that are no longer appropriate; we have worked very hard to maintain them. Now we must work equally hard and long to repair our damaged selves.

Our childhood trauma angered us. As AMACs, we directed that anger against ourselves, our families, our perpetrators, society, government, or any other authority that appeared in our lives. It was these "carry-over" feelings, as we call them, that we inflicted upon others. We had to diminish everybody and everything around us in order to equalize the comparison. How else could we be worthy to live?

What was bad felt familiar to us. Good was foreign. Most human beings are quick to recognize and accept what is most familiar, and AMACs are no exception. Our bizarre and zany expectations actually made unnatural conditions less threatening to us than wholesome and natural ones. We wouldn't share our secrets with anyone, not even a power greater than ourselves, whatever we understood such a power to be. We felt that if we told the truth about ourselves, the bogeyman would get us; no one would believe us, or we would be rejected and left alone yet again, just as we were alone and unprotected when we were being molested in childhood.

The people responsible for our safety and our care had given us a distorted understanding of adults. They abandoned, abused, and molested us. Then they blamed, criticized, and beat us. Or they just used us and then ignored us until they wanted us again for their own sick perversions. In our relationships with these people, distrust was appropriate self-protection. We could not switch off our distrust of adults, however, when we ourselves grew up.

How can we ever trust anyone? When we grew up, we became the image of those who betrayed us. How can we even trust ourselves, now that we have become adults? How can we feel comfortable being trusted by others? To say that we are caught in a dilemma is putting the pinch very mildly! No wonder we are ill at ease even when, for all practical reasons, we ought to be comfortable as adults. The effects of our childhood traumas didn't cease when the physical events ended, but colored everything that happened thereafter.

Nevertheless, when we searched ourselves, we found much good. Most of us were surprised after all these years of feeling inadequate and dysfunctional. We guarantee that, if you are sincere and honest about your recovery, you will find good in yourself too. We were born good, not bad; no child is born bad. We were taught to become what we grew up to be. We can unlearn the falsehoods that hurt us until they became habit. This realization frees us to be unselfish enough to own our problems and become selfish enough to heal.

Our recovery evolves through the workings of the AAMAC Twelve Step program. The First Step begins our journey toward recovery: We admit that we are powerless over our having been molested as children and that parts of our lives have become unmanageable. We cannot own what isn't ours. We return the responsibility for our abuse to its rightful owners, the perpetrators.

The first logical step to solving any problem is admitting that it exists. The admission entails ownership of the problem, if not its causes. Once we accept that ownership, we have the vested interest and the power to solve it. Denial only makes it worse. If we are to deal with the reality of our situation, we must be truthful with ourselves and with each other. Deceit only creates more illusions. The decision to deny or accept our life is ours to make. Though these statements seem simple, they are monuments on our journey to recovery, choices that would enhance anybody's life, not only the lives of AMACs.

From our First Step comes our first task, which is to discover who we really were and what we really are now, at any given moment. The reasoning behind this task is that our feelings fluctuate considerably and at quick intervals, but within those fluctuations, a whole person is trying to evolve. As we discover our more and less admirable characteristics, we share the results of our search with other AMACs, who share similar information with us. In this manner of sharing truth, we learn quickly and profitably. Sharing our secrets is how we conquer them. We help lead each other through self-discovery by meeting with each other and working on ourselves together. In doing so, we tend to keep an open mind. We never know where we will hear the message we need. The exercise of trust and faith in one another, coupled with our faith in a power greater than ourselves, overcomes our fear of discovery. The moment we begin to share our hidden thoughts, healing occurs. Our healthy awareness of ourselves and others like ourselves expands. Our workshops are proof that people who know the worst of us may love us anyway.

Discovering and sharing one's self is also one of our definitions of true generosity, another healing agent. Confession is good for the spirit, not only in particular religious practices, but also in a more general way, the search for higher awareness. As we see it, higher awareness is the consciousness of self and others without possessiveness or malice. The vehicle for achieving this kind of awareness could be God, truth, therapy, the workshop, AAMAC as a whole, or any kind of power that we believe to be greater than ourselves.

One thing is sure. Our sick egos must be righted, which will require every particle of our spiritual energy. No power of any proportion will make this journey for us, but neither do we have sufficient energy to make it alone. Our past has proven that fact in no uncertain terms. We needn't abandon any personal belief, if it is true belief, but must use it to its greatest potential and capacity to help us. In AAMAC, we are only as strong as our weakest member, only as sick as we are secret. We hide our secrets by denying these facts. We cannot disguise who we are unless we are also willing to accept the disguises of others. This is not blindness. It is a voluntary conspiracy with others to deny the truth by closing our eyes to it. Whenever we choose not to see what is in front of us, then we have seen anyway. We saw, we denied what we saw, and we slipped deeper into our hidden worlds, lonely and full of fear while yearning to be happy, joyous, and free.

Our Third Legacy, Recovery, is about this curious practice of self-deception. We say that for us to have sight is not the same as to see. These realizations take time. Be kind to yourself, and don't try to comprehend everything in one reading of this book. It cannot be done. Our literature requires several readings before one can think about old things in new ways and seek a true recovery. In our personal search for truth, we have had to go beyond our suffering. We must accept the responsibility for much of that suffering in adulthood. We ourselves make our decisions. We can seek help whenever we wish. We know when we feel bad. The real fact is that we played a game, with our lives and the lives of others, for so long that we no longer knew what was real. If we had ever accepted the reality of who and what we really were as AMACs, that would have required us to admit that we were in error about many of our beliefs and lifestyles.

In other words, we were complacent in our misery. When we begin to go about change, we can't yet understand how we became so disoriented. That lack of understanding blocks us from admitting our character defects and shortcomings. We sense that we are living in secrets. We sense that we fear discovery. We sense that we have living problems. We sense that we are out of sync with our inner selves and the outer world in which we play and live. For all our misnamed feelings, we blame ourselves, and invent various reasons why we feel and act as we do.

In their true light, our secrets are nothing more than a series of misunderstandings and misinterpretations about things that happened long ago. As we grow to understand this, once and for all, we become a little angry about what we have done to ourselves for all these painful years. That anger pushes us onward into discovery and helps us overcome our syndrome of being sick and tired of being sick and tired. We AMACs really know how to stick it to ourselves. If nobody else will do it, we berate ourselves. We can eventually learn to laugh at such antics.

We hid out in secrecy because we lacked understanding about ourselves and our circumstances. As we strive to understand, we become less hesitant about sharing our secrets. Not one among us can deny that our adult lives brought us only more pain. For many of us, our illusions became mental illness; we could no longer separate the real from the unreal. What appeared normal to most others seemed bizarre to us. Some of us admit that we have even done great harm to protect the secrets of our childhood past. In fact, our jails, prisons, and mental institutions are full of AMACs who lashed out blindly at society in order to protect their false illusions. Untreated, many are doomed to repeat the tragic cycle.

Consider the burden we carried as adults just to keep our secrets hidden from ourselves. If that burden were not heavy enough, consider the anxiety we felt over others' learning about them. Our early sexual experiences were horrible enough. Our own revulsion magnified the imagined reaction of others. In addition, our adult lives have been stunted. To top it all off, now we must acknowledge our own responsibility for our adulthood and recover from addiction to our assorted symptoms. All of this knowledge poses a terrible threat to any adult who was molested in childhood.

Our past has blurred our vision. We commonly labor to fix something that either already works or is hopelessly beyond repair. Our fear of discovery pushes us into blind acts of busywork. It is quite a chore to keep our minds busy enough in fantasy and labor to avoid knowing consciously what we know inside full well. We are experts at diversionary tactics; the wreckage of our lives speaks for itself. Before treatment and recovery in AAMAC, we suffered the grand delusion, no matter what tragic experiences befell us, that things would somehow change. While we ourselves went on the same, we somehow expected different results in the future.

The idea that we will someday simply step out of our negative behaviors, states of mind, and troubled lifestyles is commonplace among AMACs. How often we have thought we would have the perfect relationship, next time. We would handle life perfectly and on life's terms, next time. We would not do this thing or that thing ever again, next time. The misbegotten concept of next time is just one of the many great obsessions and illusions we AMACs harbor.

Failure has haunted us for a long time. Often we thought we couldn't do something we wanted to do because we would just mess it up anyway. We didn't go on that job interview because we wouldn't get hired anyway. We didn't study for the test because we would just fail it anyway. We thought life would be miserable anyway, no matter what we did, so why bother showing up? Our obsessions and fantasies about failure are so intense and persistent that we often hold on to them, even to the point that we're oblivious to successes! It isn't at all uncommon for an AMAC to wake up suddenly and find that he has been walking around all wrong while thinking he was headed in the right direction. When we discovered our mistaken course, we simply blamed other people, places, and things. Denial is a great shield, and we use it constantly.

For us to see ourselves as we really are and realize what we may become if we don't change is one of the great tasks for us all. We need to see ourselves in other AMACs to accomplish this chore. If we don't change direction, we will remain in our dysfunctions. We may convince ourselves otherwise, but our past speaks for itself. If we are to recover fully, we need help. Our wanting that help is another matter, even when we are asking for it. We can become Twelve Step junkies and never grow out of our problems if we are not careful. When that happens, the program becomes a mere semblance of real action, more distracting busywork, rather than a guide into recovery. Many AMACs do not even know that they are AMACs, let alone suspect that such experiences could remotely affect their lives. Together we are a living answer that gradually unfolds.

By consensus, we agree that few AMACs go through life without some kind of treatment and reach anything near their potential for happiness and freedom. Certainly none who have walked through our doors have claimed such achievement. The closest any of us came was during very short spurts of extreme highs, followed by low lows. Most of us need treatment and ongoing long-term maintenance of our lives if we hope to reach some sort of balanced emotional state of being and becoming. Many of us have experienced brief periods when our sadness subsided and the weight of our secrets faded, but, sooner or later, they returned to haunt what we had thought was a new life. We will always feel some of that old pain, but we are growing to the point where we needn't regret our past or shut it out. If we catch ourselves slipping back into denial, we know that we are also in relapse.

The bottom line for us is that we are what we think. If we can change our basic thinking, then we can change our behavior, attitudes, thoughts, and emotions. We are always changing and creating new habits anyway. We can control the results and develop ourselves in more positive ways. That is why we must have hope for those who have no hope for themselves. If we believe in ourselves, others will eventually believe as we do. There are no shortcuts; we have tried them all and are not inclined to look for any more. We must stick to the main issue of what we are and not kid ourselves about anything. Acceptance is the key to our recovery. The heart of this matter is that we are responsible for what we let happen in our adult lives. It is we who must change the things that we can and get help to change those things that we cannot seem to alter on our own.

Our goal during our recovery is to relive our experiences enough times by thinking and talking about them to distinguish the exact nature of our nonchemical addictions called obsessions. Most of us in AAMAC spend two hours a week attending a workshop and a few hours a week talking with each other on the phone. Those who apply themselves and work our entire program use our AAMAC Twelve Steps and say that it speeds recovery and helps them, especially with the Fourth and Fifth Steps. Twelve or so hours a week is what it takes at first to work the program most effectively. Since we spent twenty-four hours a day, seven days a week in our problems and dysfunctions before we joined AAMAC, we feel that our effort applied to recovery is an economical investment.

This book comes out of our own journey. What we found by banding together was good. That is our reward for courageous effort and for being selfish enough to heal. We have learned that we don't have to hurry; once we have taken our First Step, we need only continue being thorough. Our old ways of life will be with us for a long time because they are subtle and usually show themselves in erratic symptoms. We improve by degrees rather than leaps and bounds. Chances are that we already know what we are struggling to discover. Our own denial is our fundamental problem. The attitudes, behaviors, and emotions which we thought were our problems are only the symptoms of such denial.

If our hearts are right, we can come to know the difference between selfishness and generosity, busy giving and true service to others. We learn the difference between self-centeredness and true love of self in a healthy way. We learn that, by putting out false personalities, we attract false friendships and lose our proper relationship with our species and our universe. We must keep open minds and grow slowly, allowing problems to grow away, rather than trying to make them go away. Although we seldom fail in recovery if we give our best, we rarely get all that we want. This realization has taught us that getting from point A to point B is not success in AAMAC terms. We must consistently renegotiate our basic life plan with ourselves and with the people in our world as we change and grow. It is all quite simple, once we give up making life more complicated than it has to be.

Recovery is not easy, but misery as an untreated AMAC is far more difficult and painful than recovery. Our lives have improved significantly, and others see beautiful changes in us over time. For all our effort, recovery is the prize.

3

OUR PROGRAM OF RECOVERY

Truly strong people share their weaknesses.
It is from having the courage to share one's
weaknesses that a person gains real strength.
In AAMAC, we prefer that our problems
grow away rather than go away.

If we listen to the silence, we can hear the songs. The silence was within us, and not outside ourselves. If we pause to remember that there is more, then wonders open up to us. We are not in a dream. The silence was the dream. There is music everywhere. We ourselves become the words to our songs.

Whatever you may find upon these pages that you do not understand, leave it and go on. That place will always be your new beginning, waiting until you are ready to deal with it. Do not hurry. Much of what we are writing here is knowledge that we already knew somewhere inside, without knowing that we knew.

Whatever is secret in the universe is only a discovery waiting to be made. Together we can overcome whatever we do not like about ourselves. Whatever our problems, with adequate time to heal, proper help, honesty about ourselves, and courage to work on ourselves with each other, we can solve most of our problems. We participate in AAMAC because we want to improve our lives. We also want to assist others. Nobody makes us come to AAMAC, and nobody makes us stay. We are our own free moral agents, here because we want to be here!

AAMAC claims no responsibility for anyone's success or failure. To do so would rob us of our proper rewards for our journey through self. Our individual successes and failures in our own recovery are what motivate us to the next plane of recovery. For that reason, we must experience our own just dues and rewards.

Once involved in AAMAC, we felt that we were upon a healing journey, exactly what we had been missing, or aborting, for so long. The moment we made contact with other adults who had been molested as children, we anticipated new and wonderful experiences, and we have not been disappointed. We found the courage to feel the depths of our sorrows in order to understand how to relieve our burden and pain. While practicing our old ways of life, we continued to formulate negative beliefs and attitudes. Though we have decided to take control of our lives, we retain the remnants of our trauma-ridden past. We are therefore cautious and restrained in much of what we think and do. Few of us realize at the beginning that, once we overcome some of our initial problems, changes that we never dreamed possible follow as a matter of natural course. Our freedom from the bondage of our past is not only possible, but probable!

We are trying to step out of our nightmare and enter a new reality. Should we feel guilty about our AMAC past? No, but most of us do anyway. We need only admit our shame and guilt and be honest about it with ourselves and other AMACs. In sharing our secrets, we usually find that everyone else has experienced similar failures and disappointments anyway; some secret! The guilt that we have felt all these years is just another carry-over feeling that we didn't know how to change. It results from our having blamed ourselves for being molested as children. We suspect that some of this guilt owes to our pleasure conflicts in childhood, when we felt sick about what was happening to us and simultaneously enjoyed the erotic feelings that awoke prematurely in our innocent bodies. We could not possibly comprehend this confusion as young children.

As adults, we have been seeking fulfillment to replace the void we felt in our childhood. Although it is true that in adult life we wanted what we wanted, few of us expected what we wound up with. Most of us have been following lonely, endless paths. Nobody in AAMAC ever has to be alone again, regardless of the past! Nor does anyone ever have to be afraid again in the same old way.

From the promise of tomorrow, we derive hope. The combination of experience and hope gives us energy to stay in today and do what we must to maintain balance. We take heart from old philosophy and new experience, which we express in our credo:

- From courage comes change.
- From change comes wisdom.
- From wisdom comes acceptance.
- From acceptance comes understanding.
- From combinations of all these things comes the ability to forgive.
- From this forgiving comes the healing that brings us serenity.
- From this serenity comes the substance that provides us with something to give away to others.

The process summarized in this statement of our belief has enabled many of us to build healthy relationships and correct the troubled lives we are used to leading. Because we have been working to develop and nurture love and empathy, we have enough to give away, understanding at last that sharing these feelings with others is normal. We realize now that we are more than our gender roles and that men and women share common ground. We therefore don't need literature specifically directed to males or females. Because we have met and learned to trust both men and women in our workshops, we have come to see members of the other sex as human beings like ourselves, with more similarities than differences.

One of our tragic flaws was our obsession with the delusion of uniqueness. We thought that no one else ever lived through such experiences as ours; no one else ever felt such emotions. Workshops including members of both sexes allow us to see that we are all in this together, we are people after all. We have discovered that men and women both feel the same basic feelings.

Looking for commonalities rather than differences means freedom from having to judge others harshly, as we used to do. Our habitual harsh judgments were in fact self-judgments turned inside out. We certainly felt different from most people we have known during our lives. Believing that we, and only we, were tainted and corrupt, we expected perfection in others. Our impossible expectations of society and humanity came from denial. Differences separate people from people, and that is exactly what our perceptions did.

When we accept others as themselves, it is we who begin to heal. We must forgive and accept ourselves as well as others. We cannot experience a complete recovery without doing so. We are organisms seeking the fulfillment of our nature, like all other living creatures. To be friends with others, we must first be friends with ourselves. We must learn to appreciate ourselves and the fact that we are alive.

We knew before we joined AAMAC that it was not going to be a place where we could hide. At the beginning, we had so many fears that we couldn't separate them. It isn't the number of our fears that matters, but the fact that they all sprout from the same root: the fear of discovery. We are not magically fearless now, but we are learning to live with our fears. Some of the most difficult acts for us have always been working with others, participating in healthy activities, following suggestions or directions, and being open about ourselves. The origin of these difficulties is fear. By working together, we learn why we are afraid; understanding the source melts away much of that fear.

As AMACs, we suffer from many unpredictable emotions. It isn't unusual for our minds to be crowded with thoughts one moment and almost blank the next. Our calm gives way to excitement in seconds, for no obvious reason. We know now, however, that fantasies and events that echo our childhood abuse cause such sudden shifts. In contrast to this instability, we may sometimes be immobilized for long periods of time by confusion, frustration, doubts, or deep depression. This surely is a hell of a way to live!

Although we may have found only chaos and isolation until now, we can live more productively. A happier way of life is natural. Happiness is not a great privilege granted by divine decision. If we take action to change specific flaws in ourselves, other changes will occur less painfully with time. We try not to rush ourselves, knowing how deeply our old lives are embedded in our innermost selves.

Although we simplify and focus, we try not to become obsessed with working on just one issue. We tend to neglect the overall picture. We get hooked on working out a conflict and forget to implement the results in a more satisfying life. Some of us solve a problem and continue to live ineffectively, even though we continue to participate in the workshops. That happens when we have all the right answers for all the wrong reasons, using the program to reinforce our dysfunctions rather than to recover fully. To do so is to win a battle or two, but lose the war.

We must grow slowly and be thorough in our reasoning if we are to avoid such pitfalls. Talking a program is one thing. Working a program is an entirely different matter. An open mind is the channel to change. Openness requires us to consider anything that enters our consciousness; to try not to bury memory and banish thought; to discover and probe deeper; to realize, recognize, and discard; to listen and share our most intimate thoughts with other AMACs.

As we begin to change, new feelings emerge. We often talk about feeling a different kind of loneliness. Our old sense of isolation was more a feeling than a fact; we could and usually did feel alone in a crowd. This sense of loss is similar to the emotional devastation in the first days after a close relationship is broken off for some reason.

"Soft loneliness" is not the same harsh feeling of isolation AMACs usually feel, but more like the melancholy one feels mourning the loss of a loved one and finally accepting that he is gone. Perhaps we miss our old selves in subtle ways; even though we were unhealthy, we were familiar with ourselves. Perhaps we are mourning the death of that old dysfunctional friend. Perhaps we are accepting that our childhood was stolen, though we may still reclaim parts of it. Acceptance of unavoidable facts is a relief. Surrendering to reality lets us leave the tragedy behind.

We try to feel the difference between the old, harsh, alienated loneliness, that sense of utter isolation from the universe, and this softer loneliness, which feels natural, as if it belongs to us. We search our memory and compare this calm aloneness with other kinds of feelings, such as the emptiness just after we were molested. Back then, we felt that our selves had been lost, stolen from us. We were helpless, with no one to protect us from further harm. We became addicted to reliving that grief.

Now, with a new emotion in our consciousness, we have something fresh and different to compare with that old grief. Once we can discriminate between these two different feelings, our softer sense of solitude replaces the sadness that we have suffered for so long. The new emotion is more than mourning. It is union with life, another foreign sensation for an AMAC. It is the absence of old conflicts. We let it flow naturally, coming and going as it will. Our solitude can heal and reward us. What comes naturally does not carry with it destructive pain and suffering. Instead, it brings the clarity of growth.

This new emotion is another of those feelings that we always knew, but never brought to the surface before. We used to repress it out of fear, thinking it strange or weird, feeling unnatural because of it, as we felt about many of our healthier emotions. Feelings are the way our bodies and minds communicate with one another and the way we respond to our perceptions of the world around us. Now, we rarely feel outcast unless we have alienated ourselves from the program and our recovery.

Loneliness is one of the many problems that trouble everybody. We all seek relief from the pressures, anxieties, and boredom of life in modern society, but these problems appear more pronounced in AMACs. We have spent our lives trying futilely to escape our pain. The very methods we used to escape from the stresses normal to everybody, and those that are familiar only to AMACs, caused us more problems.

Over the years, we integrated our escape techniques with our other negative attitudes, emotions, and behaviors, and they became habitual. We usually chose the most painful ways of life, rather than overcome our fear and reveal our secrets. We were hooked on feeling bad about ourselves and everything else. These obsessions, or compulsory habits of thought, are what block our vision.

It is we who raise and lower the bridge into society. We have the right to do so. The only force that prevents our joining society is ourselves. We are responsible for our actions. It is we who never ask the question, but invent the answer in order to stay in our secrets. It is we who couple the need to know with the fear of knowing, for knowing confronts us with the options for change.

We do good things and don't even know it. We do and see things for negative reasons, always expecting the obvious negative results for our negative efforts. We trained ourselves to see failure. Nobody likes to be wrong, especially AMACs; if things turn out well for us, we sometimes find a way to make them negative. Even after initial recovery, compliments often embarrass and disturb us. If someone tells us that we're handsome, pretty, gifted, capable, or talented, or if anyone hints that we own any other possible virtue, we deny it. We are compelled to feel ashamed of ourselves.

We suggest that readers make up their own list of damaging responses and then write how such responses affect their lives, using the exercise on the next page and a separate piece of paper. Be painstakingly honest thinking through this exercise. It may turn out to be the best thing we can can do for ourselves. Don't complicate it with a lot of unnecessary words and justification. Simply start with the partial list we have made and go on from there.

ADDICTION, OBSESSION, OR HABIT	EFFECT ON MY LIFE
Denial	Interferes with my relationship. Causes me to stay defensive. Makes others angry at me. Stops my own recovery. Covers my inferiority feelings and complexes. Helps me to keep lying to myself about me. Helps me remain unhealthy.

Self-justification:

Fear:

Anger:

Rage:

Hate:

Vengeance:

Sex:

Alcohol:

Other Drugs:

To uncover our addictions, obsessions, or just plain bad habits is to discover true and meaningful ways to change them. We simply flip them over and do the opposite. If we quit committing an action, we instantly change. When someone gives us a compliment, we say a simple "thank you," rather than offer a long account of the ways we might have done better. Having done a job to someone else's satisfaction qualifies us to accept his approval graciously, rather than look for our worst. We try not to step on somebody else's efforts to express appreciation. On the other hand, we don't expect a ticker tape parade. When we are wrong, we promptly admit it. When others think we're wrong, we ask them why they think so. If we don't know the answer to a question, we say so. We have nothing to fear but our own dishonesty. Discovering our flaws is how we gain insight into changing ourselves and our behavior.

When we forgive others, we begin to heal. The energy we gain from forgiving something we disliked, we can now apply to forgiving ourselves as well. Self-forgiveness seemed to be impossible to many of us, but we have learned in AAMAC that this dream is possible, after all. Even more surprising is the speed with which most of us reach this level of forgiveness. We actually learn to feel comfortable with feeling comfortable, rather than suspect trouble when things go well.

When we analyze our experience, we find that the form of our molestation influences our dysfunction. If there was raw brutality involved, we may lean toward domestic violence. If there were token rewards, we may lean toward prostitution. If we felt pleasure, we may lean toward promiscuity. If we suffered a lot of physical pain, we may be frigid or impotent. If we were molested by someone of our own sex, we may overcompensate our masculinity or femininity by rebelling in some way. Perhaps we cannot tolerate one steady relationship, and we experience divorce after divorce because of the same repeated dysfunction. This paragraph should bring much discussion in any AAMAC workshop.

But now it is time to forgive ourselves for the ways by which we have molested our own adult lives and disrupted our well-being. Who decides where is the best place to start? We think it wise to begin by staying in the present of our recovery and accepting things as they are at the moment. We first reorganize our negative thought patterns to avoid working our way into new problems. We can also set some priorities and sort out the good and the bad in our old way of life. We can consciously look for positive elements in everyday life. This is a time to explore friend-ships all around us; while we struggle to find a new footing, we benefit from delaying any exclusive new romance until we find stability. We need to let our lives flow and be leery of imposing expectations and illusions on ourselves. Most important, we try to solve our problems one at a time. This provides us with greater clarity.

Nothing alive is ever problem-free. None of us was very happy at the beginning of the program about the effort it would take for us to set our lives straight. We knew we would have to search our selves; bring down false pride; own our problems and accept responsibility for our adult actions; admit our faults and overcome them; and repair or abandon our dysfunctional relationships. These are major transformations, none of them painless or easy, but we knew that we must either transform our-selves or continue in our suffering.

Each of us decided for ourselves, no more grief! Other AMACs who had resolved their problems with reasonable success gave us hope that we could do the same. We were apprehensive about the undertaking, but we were not alone. We could actually participate in our recovery and say a great deal about what would happen to us. By observing those who had gone before us, those who came after us, and those going through recov-ery with us, we witness our own past, present, and future whenever we wish. We no longer seek rescue, but are fixing ourselves. Our rewards are sweet because we have secured them with active effort.

This is how recovery is supposed to work. Others can guide us and walk with us, and our spiritual base can provide energy, but nobody can do it for us.

4

THERE IS MORE

*As we reach each new plane in our recovery,
we are amazed to find that we experience a
new state of infancy. Recovery is a journey
from infancy to infancy. Life itself is a journey from infancy to infancy, repeated recovery from each new state of uncertainty.*

Will we rule over the problems, or will the problems rule us? The choice
is ours. Our AAMAC Twelve Steps, Twelve Traditions, and Five Legacies of Recovery and Service give us insight into what we can do about
our problems. These suggestions enhanced our lives when we applied
them and followed their path of self-discovery and understanding.

If this program seems not to work for some AMACs, no one is at
fault. We can only guarantee that our own lives have improved immeasurably as we benefited from these precepts and ideas. While AAMAC
resembles other Twelve Step programs in some respects, we also depart
from the model when our experience shows us that another way works
better. Our malady differs from those at the center of other recovery
groups, and we need to have open minds.

Although a long road still lies ahead, we feel happier now than we
ever felt before. Had we not undertaken willingly to participate in our
treatment and recovery, we are certain that we would not be this far along.
More remains for us to do, to think about, and to unlearn, but now we
can hope and trust in our personal resources as we never could before.

For good reason, we value openness, free expression, trust, and confidentiality, and insist upon closed meetings for AMACs only. Idle gos-
sip, which generally results from premature judgments of others,
endangers the well-being of our AAMAC society. It is imperative that we

speak well of each other outside our society and that we not judge another because of what he has revealed. We could never summon the courage to tell the truth without some confidence that the truth would never leave the workshop room.

Remembering our own initial anxiety, we know the discomfort new members feel when they arrive at our door. That is why someone will be here to greet you. Rest assured, you needn't explain why you are here beyond stating that you are an AMAC, or that you're trying to find out whether you are. We know that you are searching for more than just a quick way out if you have read our book to this point. We also know that you have courage and the capacity to change. We know that you have some hope and the ability to love and care. We know these things because you would not come to an AAMAC workshop unless these attributes had enabled you to visit. We are not so naive as to think that you necessarily know or believe these wonderful things about yourself. You will learn more about your virtues, as we did, during your recovery. At your heart is a desire for peace. May you find it here in AAMAC as we have.

The full responsibility for recovery rests with the individual and depends upon sincerity and effort. Without your wanting us and what we offer, there is no motive to change. Without personal responsibility for recovery, there is no personal reward; how can one be rewarded for something she did not do? Without accepting ownership of our own problems, how can we recover from them?

Our ways are neither painless nor easy, but they are true and fair. The path will be harder for some of us than for others. We ask of our members only what we ourselves are willing to share, within the scope of our lives as AMACs. Our personal rewards are our earnings from the hard and honest labor of examining our innermost selves. Without profound desire for our own and our friends' recovery, we would probably fail. WE ARE SERIOUS ABOUT OUR RECOVERY. We will accept nothing less. We come here from every walk of life; to us collectively, there is nothing new under the sun. We know we have conned our way through life, and can smile at the cons of others. New members can count on us to be truthful about our impressions of ourselves.

We are all in various stages of recovery and are susceptible to every human behavior, emotion, and frailty. Open minds necessitate open communication. AMACs new to our workshop are probably disillusioned from lifelong disappointment. We mustn't forget our purpose and lose ourselves in personalities. We guard against further disillusioning others, our way of loving them in their best interest. We therefore tell each other the truth about ourselves, in the process sharing strength, experience, and trust, hoping that all who stay in AAMAC will do likewise. If these are qualities that you seek for yourself, then you will be happy among us. We don't try to save the world; if you want us, you must seek us out, or start a workshop in your area.

Our principles come from a well of diverse knowledge and life experience. We cannot and will not try to force anyone to change his state of mind. We claim only that we can enhance your awareness of yourself, your problems, and your potential, and help you change the way you view the world. Beyond that, the task of growth belongs to each individual. Take what you want and leave what you think does not apply to you.

Our new awareness gives us energy and greater desire for change, but the road is not smooth. We experience many transition periods, gaps between what we were and what we are becoming. During these shifts, our emotions are likely to be unstable, with lofty highs and deep lows. The resulting discomfort tempts us to quit our recovery and return to the more familiar old self. All we can say to this uneasiness is, don't quit. Don't quit before the new you emerges. At this point in our recovery, we want change but are frustrated and confused by new feelings. These feelings, it turns out, result from our already having changed! We are always the last to know, because it takes time for us to receive new reflections of ourselves from the mirror of other people's responses to us. It takes time for them to accept the new persons we have become and react in a positive way. The old addictions and obsessions with low self-esteem try to creep back in. We often imagine that we are failing when actually we are growing. Problems magnify because we are at the brink of decision. Will we quit and go backward, or will we continue and move forward?

Over time, then, we experience many new commitments to truth and freedom, until we have emerged as new people. Our peace speaks for itself to those who wish to hear. Sorrows change into soft loneliness, fading memories which are insignificant in the context of our whole lives. Fears no longer control us, but become fleeting thoughts. Each day, we feel more hope as possibilities open for us.

At the same time, we resist the urge to become grand. We did not come to AAMAC to learn how to walk on water or find Mr. or Mrs. Wonderful. We have wrought pain enough to ourselves and others involved with us. How we treat each other as we deal with our particular problems in the AAMAC society can be therapeutic if we mean well. We can also be destructive if our motives are false. AAMAC is not a place to seek revenge, but a place for compassion and understanding.

Sooner or later the question arises, How do we see each other? Is it through our smiles, how we walk, our voices, or the color of our skin? Do we look at one another and see reflections of ourselves? Do we see others as they really are or as we want them to appear? Do we see only attributes which we ourselves lack? Are we simply each others' teachers? By what gauge do we measure anything? Are we victims of our own creations and beliefs? Do we see each other or do we simply mirror one another's needs and wants? These are lifelong questions. The answers change as we grow.

We are more than just flesh, bone, and physical desire. WE ARE FEELINGS, the spirit's whisperings into the ear of our minds. The spirit tries to persuade us, in a gentle way, to be kind to ourselves and seek happiness through truth. The key to our living worse or better lives is the way we choose to see things, how we think about the world. If we do not want to see things in a more positive way, then nothing can change for the better. It is our state of mind that makes the difference. Today is either a reflection of our past or the beginning of our future. It is a matter of deciding which it will be and then following through to realize our vision.

Our program of recovery is not easy, but our lives as untreated AMACs were far more difficult! We are worth our effort. The world is not going to change for us, but we can change ourselves. We have learned that it is better for us to try to do the best that we can rather than the most that we can. Busy minds don't necessarily recover. We can become so busy that we merely collect information and wind up with no time to apply our new knowledge in our daily lives. We can become so addicted to recovery that we forget to recover. Ignoring families and our other obligations or responsibilities is not recovering, even if we neglect them in the name of recovery. That is not to say that we shouldn't take time for ourselves. But we must learn to balance our own and others' needs and pace our days accordingly. Quality is what we are about. More is not necessarily better.

As we recover, real problems in the world clarify. New conflicts arise in us about ourselves, our past, and the present. Looking about us at society, we see our most trusted leaders caught up in corruption and scandal. We see mass violence, rampant substance abuse, and betrayal at a world level. We live in the shadow of nuclear destruction, environmental pollution, financial exploitation, and spiritual degeneration. Low wages and high costs make many of us poor. Such realities dampen our spirits; now that we see ourselves more clearly, we turn to society for encouragement, and instead find imperfection everywhere.

We must realize that life has the meaning we give it. We can grow only to the point of seeing bad for bad and good for good. What we choose to dwell upon can drag us down or build us up. Though much of our modern world is in disorder, we can still put our personal world in order and live a better, happier way of life. What the world chooses to do to itself doesn't matter much to our personal recovery. We have our own sickness to deal with. Now, choosing to heal ourselves, we needn't participate in the sickness of others. We don't have to be part of the problem, but can be part of the answer. Merely by healing, we shall have made the world a better place for everyone. And we must be careful not to be too critical of the world; not everyone has had the good fortune of a program like AAMAC to guide her.

We have discovered many new truths about ourselves while recovering from our hopeless states of mind. We see now, for instance, that we expected goodness from life without effort. We wanted money, prestige, warmth, empathy, and respect, but we didn't feel any obligation of generosity in our own relationships with others. When we were receiving such bounty, we often didn't recognize it. Most of us never had such positive experiences as children and therefore grew up blind to them, only imagining such wonders. We so badly wanted comfort, and pleasure, and status that we got hooked on the wanting and failed to recognize when such things looked us in the face. Generosity and gratitude are difficult for most AMACs. Since others wanted things from us and took them from us in childhood, we assume as adults that our friends and relatives will make unacceptable demands and offer nothing in return. Our selfishness and self-centeredness was set long before we could understand it.

Now we try to practice both giving and receiving, wanting what we have, especially when we find that we may not have what we want.

We have discovered that we are pretty much what we think. We were ruled by fear, illusion, and false values. We never realized that we thought and saw everything through the distorting lens of childhood abuse, which caused our adult pessimism. We thought that everyone else hid behind masks as we did. While others grew up with dreams, we lived in real nightmares. It isn't surprising that we didn't want to know our faults. We feared what we might discover. After all, we know our thoughts and feelings, while others can only guess at them. And we feared finding out worse things about ourselves than we already knew. We were just trying to pass for normal, but we didn't know what normal was.

AMACs struggle to accept life in a practical, positive way. We have spent too much time in daydreams; our fantasies distract us from our painful secrets and feelings, protecting us from the necessity to deal with them. All of us relapse easily into such old habits, another reason that we go after quality recovery rather than quantities of busyness.

One of our most painful obsessions is the possibility of passing our trouble on to a new generation of children. Although some AMACs become perpetrators themselves, more of us destroy ourselves than molest children. We are more likely as parents to either overprotect our own children or to push them away, fearing to hold them too close in a doomed attempt to recapture our lost childhood. Most AMAC parents we know admit that they lack feelings of affection for one or more of their children. Since nobody showed us healthy affection, we didn't know how to give it to our children. The fact is that we were usually so obsessed with ourselves that we simply didn't fully recognize that other people were involved in our lives. We even feared our own love for others, dreading that it might be dysfunctional. As we discuss such topics as self-obsession, and our manner of raising children, and society, we discover the reasons for these curious behaviors and traits. We know now that we were never taught how to be nurturing in any kind of relationship. That insight alone results in change.

These are not statements of blame. Such clear and honest vision of our common shortcomings allow us gradually to shed our rigid old reflexes, replacing them with new skills. This natural flow relieves our loss, filling the voids left by our outgrown behavior. We are well aware of the ugly feelings that we harbored inside ourselves; once, we accepted those ugly feelings as part of us. Nobody gives up anything deeply embedded in personality unless there is something of greater worth to take its place. Our cup of peace must fill if our cup of bitterness is to empty. That is just the way it works.

In imagination, AMACs inflate or diminish what we are, denying our real selves and a better way of life. Confronting the truth about one's character, the better parts as well as the worse, is vital to anybody's emotional maturity and freedom. We are learning to think better of ourselves. It is amazing how this positive frame of mind heals us. We have the power to choose how to think. If we choose not to think well of ourselves, the alternative is thinking ill. Is that not simple and profound? Our own kindness and friendliness enables us to see ourselves in a new light. Growing self-esteem frees us for more active social lives. Seeing our self-respect, others accept us.

Self-discovery brings the ultimate realization that, as adults, we are responsible for our own actions and our lives in general. It is we who own our beings and decide what we will become. We are not tenants living in our bodies; we are the landlords. We feel our pain. We suffer from our fears. We pay the price for our actions. We hide our secrets. We experience our own death in life. It is we ourselves, then, who must act to improve our lot. We pay the price for our wrongs and shortcomings, but we also pick up the paychecks and rewards.

In AAMAC, the process of revelation is gradual enough that we can accept it. We hope that, after reading this far, you have already experienced some relief from your own guilt and pain if you are an AMAC like us. If you are not, we hope we have helped you understand us better. If you entirely disagree with us, we hope that you find what you are searching for in some other type of recovery. Peace be with you.

5

RETURNING THE PAST

We are the sum of all that we have ever been.
We can change ourselves by learning how to
think about the past in new ways.

Nothing that happens to us goes unnoticed. All memories are recorded somewhere in us, even though we may not be aware of them. Whether our memories soothe us or torment and haunt us, we own the past. If we are suffering from a remembered experience, then we are clearly responsible to resolve the issues that continue to harm us. But what of the memories that we have hidden from ourselves?

We may think that such memories sleep in dark corners of our minds, but memories do not sleep. They continuously churn, like currents in an ocean; the waters of our memories flow through us, affecting all that we are and will be. Upon this embodied record of our lives, we base our reality. Insight from the past illuminates our present condition and enables us to plan the future. We never really forget; we merely choose to think that we have forgotten.

What is this silent and invisible memory that some call the unconscious? Is it friend or foe? Should we fear it or should we discover its contents? Is it a monster hidden deep; should we skirt it on tiptoe and let it lie? We think not. Our subconscious mind is a natural part of our natural selves. We can never unexperience our past. We were present in childhood, and our bodies heard, smelled, felt, and reacted to all that they experienced, just as they do now. We cannot think consciously and rationally about some things our bodies know. About these things, we think and remember with our sensations and emotions.

Most of us who come to AAMAC sooner or later evict the past by examining it in the strong light of the present day. If the past causes present pain or undermines the future, we are responsible to change. We can voluntarily examine memories of our perpetrators in order to see how childhood trauma rules our adult lives.

This return to the past is a very important part of our self-discovery. But what about the adult who has blocked her past out of conscious memory ... almost? Are we responsible for straightening out our lives, even if we cannot quite remember what happened? We believe that we do have that duty to ourselves. If we are having problems in adulthood, and if we want to change, we must seek help and take whatever measures are necessary to grow out of our destructive reaction. Knowing that our bodies remember what happened in infancy and childhood, we assume that, if anyone suspects that he was molested, chances are that he was, and he is entitled to membership in AAMAC. Mere feelings are grounds for looking deeper into the past.

Collectively, we in AAMAC are a memory! Whatever we do not recall from our own past, other AMACs bring to the surface, to blessed consciousness, by sharing their own past. Together we carry the torch that lights the way down an otherwise dark path leading to the secrets we have kept from ourselves. We have always sought people, places, or things to fill in the void that we carried inside, feeling somehow incomplete. When they could not do so, we blamed them for our emptiness. Without realizing what we were doing, we made the innocent friends and family in our present lives stand in to take some of the blame for the perpetrators who actually harmed us. Now our AAMAC friends really can help us to fill our own emptiness, by guiding the way to consciousness, filling the gaps with the substantial memory of real events.

We can support one another while we sort ourselves out. After being in AAMAC for some time, one AAMAC member confronted her brother, who had sexually molested and assaulted her in childhood. When she returned from her visit with him, she was quite a different person! It was an amazing thing to see. She had found the courage to do what she thought impossible. For the rest of us, she has described one of the most meaningful experiences of her life:

I FACED MY PERPETRATOR

The horror of being molested in childhood has stayed with me throughout my life. It is not an experience that one easily forgets. Try as I may to forget it, something or someone always reminds me of this nightmare. Those horrible memories have gone through my mind, over and over, for years. After an AAMAC meeting, I decided to face my brother with what he had done to me. Another perpetrator, my uncle, was dead now, but I could still personally hand over to my brother the responsibility for injuring me.

For over twenty-two years, I had longed to confront my uncle and my brother, who is six years older than I. I had carried my secrets and protected the rotten bastards for too long, always explaining to myself that I couldn't expose them for fear of hurting my parents. As I think about it now, though, I believe that I myself wanted to keep their crimes a secret. I was afraid of threats from my brother or even physical harm. I also feared what I might do to him once I started to unload my feelings! My emotions were so confused that I buried everything, the experiences, the emotional aftermath, everything.

As I see my actions more clearly now, I was repeating the old hurt to my self by keeping the secret. I was the person who had suffered the damage! Enough is enough! My brother not only stole my childhood from me; he also haunted every moment of my subsequent life. NO MORE! My husband and I had planned to visit my family back in Colorado. I had a gut feeling that I was ready to take care of this old business and to put this perpetual nightmare out of my mind and into my brother's, where it belonged.

During the trip, I was really afraid and nervous, with innumerable mixed emotions. I thought many times that I wanted to chicken out one more time. "What if he hits me?" I thought. "What if I scratch his eyes out? What if my mother and father get involved?" I thought a lot about slogans I had learned in another recovery program. They revived my courage, and I was able to release this matter with love. I had the tools to do this job that had waited for twenty-two painful, long years.

The talks that I had with my brother about his assault on me went very well. I will never forget the look on his face, the hurt that we both felt, and the crying we both did. We held each other close, and he told me that he had paid for what he had done through every day of his life. He said that he felt so ashamed. He only wished that it had never happened. He just kept saying, over and over, "I'm so sorry."

I asked why he had done it, and he really had no answer other than to say, "It was just childhood bullshit." There were four of us kids that I know he molested. He needs help, and I told him so. I also asked him whether he had been molested as a child, and he told me it was none of my damned business. He didn't realize it, but he had given me the answer to my question. I am sure that someone molested him too.

After I had confronted my brother, my father confronted me about the molestation. It took a great deal of courage for me to talk about it with him. Whom would he believe? My brother, after all, was his most precious son. Suddenly, it no longer mattered to me whether my father believed me. It felt so good finally to be able to tell my parents about this deep, dark secret which has haunted my life. I just let it all go! Now that the secret is out, my perpetrator can start paying his own price and absorb the hurt that I have until now carried in my heart.

These deep, deep secrets that we hide eat us up and destroy us mentally, physically, and spiritually. I still feel some love for my brother, but there will always be this anger in me that, at times, is ready to explode. That is why I have decided to continue attending the AAMAC workshop meetings, letting go and letting God. I am recovering. I have a long road to travel, but most of the worst is now behind me.

I am a very grateful AAMAC member. I thank God (my Higher Power), my husband, and all of my wonderful friends in AAMAC. I also thank my other Program and friends there for all of their support, love, and help in making my new life better. It would not have been possible for me to go through this ordeal without all the people who understand me. There is help for others who are still hurting and keeping the secret. It takes a lot of courage to walk through the doors of AAMAC and admit that you were molested as a child. It takes further courage to face your perpetrator. It was hard for me, too; as the saying goes, however, "A long journey begins with one single step." Without the help of AAMAC in confronting my perpetrator, I might have killed him, along with myself. Since I faced him and returned this horrible past to its rightful owner, I have experienced unimaginable relief. I feel reborn!

To you who are still hurting, try to have faith, courage, and strength. AAMAC places you on the road to recovery. I love all of you, and my heart is with you.

Some of us accompanied the author of this testimony on her own road through recovery and had the moving experience of witnessing her healing. We hope that those who want to confront their perpetrators as she did will reach out to us for support. For any number of reasons, however, many AMACs will never be able to do so. For them too, we will be here, and we care. The fact that we understand one another in a special way bonds and unifies us. We know that no courage comes out unless there is a need to exercise it. That we care is our personal expression of gratitude for the gifts so freely given to us in AAMAC. Our house is never too full.

In order to return the past to its rightful owners, those who blighted our lives, we practice openness, hoping once we have revealed our secrets never to slide again into the fear of being discovered. Whereas we once chose the discomfort of avoiding life, now we choose the comfort of living among our peers in society, not only as AMACs, but as people. The moment we had entrusted one confidante with a true account of our former dishonesty, we had laid the groundwork for a better, happier way of life. You will not see any of us wearing white robes and halos, but we have gradually learned not to do many of the things we know are destructive to ourselves and others.

We have also given up feeling guilty for the most part. For one thing, we have unburdened ourselves of the responsibility for the wrongs others committed against us. In our present lives, moreover, we are consciously abandoning the rutted patterns of behavior which caused us an appropriate guilt. We give our lives value by observing them closely and discussing our perceptions honestly with fellow laborers in our workshop. Our future is in our own hands now. Our hearts are full of love, unity, and service to others. We care. We stand on our own two feet, turning to each other for moral support and guidance. We are basically good people, responsible above all else for our own adult lives. We are reasonably comfortable and reasonably happy because we no longer look outside ourselves for someone else to blame for our troubles. It was the prospect of this happiness that motivated us to resolve our problems and differences quickly.

We have learned the hard way that if a person doesn't try to understand what is going on in her life, any kind of problem can overwhelm her. It is usually we ourselves who obstruct our path. Since our heads go where we go, we cannot escape ourselves, try as we may.

It is impossible, of course, to avoid the stresses, strains, and hurts of normal human experience, but life needn't be perfect to be fairly comfortable. If we are not in charge of our direction, then somebody else is. Living passively gets us off the hook of responsibility for daily life, of course, and provides a ready target to blame for our failures. When we shrug off our duty to ourselves, we are still living in the shadow of the perpetrator, the ghost of our childhood helplessness and shame which we have carried over to adulthood. But such a life, which denies us the credit for our own accomplishments, is hardly living. We did whatever was necessary to give others that power over our lives, and we must do whatever is necessary to reclaim it.

The sense of our own powerlessness, the feeling that we are perpetual victims, has always been a problem for us. We suffer from many such illusions. We delude ourselves that, if we can find a way not to accept the responsibility for living, then someday our lives will be magically painless. This delusion rests upon the conviction that other people do not suffer, that life for everybody else is easy, handed to them on a silver platter. We must face the fact that life is difficult—for everybody. There is no defense against normal human suffering, whether it be the pangs of childbirth, the embarrassment of unemployment, or the insecurity of undertaking new challenges. But we can minimize normal human woe by taking charge of the problems we are able to solve.

All AMACs enter adulthood with some degree of immaturity; we have, after all, avoided risks, the life experiences that would have enabled us to work through particular stages in our growth. So we find ourselves stuck in symptoms, in depression, sexual hang-ups, alcoholism, dysfunctional relationships with relatives and spouses, friction with our children, or mired in other daunting problems that seem in themselves to be the primary cause of our grief. When we begin to treat our childhood sexual abuse as the primary problem instead, and see these other issues as the predictable outgrowth of that soul-shattering experience, then we can begin to put the pieces back together again.

That has been our experience as individuals and as a society. When others join us in this enterprise, they partake of the wisdom that grows out of a community's shared experience. That helps our new members. What they often don't realize, however, is that our helping one another is also healing, somehow empowering us, strengthening our sense of ourselves. Returning the past to its rightful owners is a lifelong undertaking, and our AAMAC society is the place for long-term challenges and lifelong friends.

6

FAMILIES OF AMAC (FAMAC)

*To try renegotiating a changing relationship
risks failure. Not to try renegotiating guar-
antees failure.*

When their awareness of self and others grows, AMACs inevitably begin
to change. We need tools to maintain the change in order to prevent our
relapse into old destructive ways. Our relatives and friends must change
with us and grow along new lines, or conflict ensues. Sometimes we even
outgrow one another. These situations emerge naturally from the recovery process, which can unsettle and threaten close relationships and leave
a spouse or close friend feeling abandoned and alienated. Our loved ones
may suffer a blow to self-esteem, feeling that they have somehow failed.
The stress magnifies situational problems and wears on everybody.
Spouses sometimes blame the program for their feelings of inadequacy
and helplessness.

Such major change as we undergo in AAMAC necessarily entails
change in the relationships which evolved while our personalities were
distorted by shame and secrecy. Families and friends of AMACs need to
work on themselves as individuals in order to adjust to the changes in
some kind of mutual harmony. The survival of the relationships will
depend upon the individual work they do on themselves, and not just on
the AMACs' recovery.

Before an AMAC reveals his childhood abuse to relatives and friends,
clusters of symptoms have usually indicated dysfunction. They may have
evolved subtly and slowly over years, and they may look like something
else, such as depression or alcoholism. They can be lethal to any kind of
relationship. Families and friends who have remained in what seem like
dysfunctional relationships with AMACs can deal with their feelings of

betrayal and hurt, and their desire for retribution, by going to work on themselves. They need to recognize and accept their own dysfunctional characteristics that have developed from coping with such difficulty and to take responsibility for their own lives.

The question "How?" yields answers without blaming anyone. "How did I play a part in this dysfunctional relationship? How did my own actions and reactions drive us apart? How am I not as great as I used to think I was?" These are the kinds of issues Families of AMACs (FAMACs) must deal with if we are all to grow together. Having chosen to stay in a relationship with an AMAC, families and friends are responsible for their part in it.

Together our memory is complete. We can lead each other safely on this journey through self, by caring and sharing our own experience. We are the way. We must search ourselves and our ailing relationships and recall things that we have tried to forget—the depression and despair, the silence and separation, the sudden shifts from unity to disharmony. In AMACs, anger-rage-hate cycles arise from nowhere, last from moments to days, and go away as though they had never happened. Fears, feelings of rejection, and unhappiness randomly occur. In the effort to adjust to such behavior swings, the entire family eventually takes on many of these manifested symptoms and becomes dysfunctional, as a whole and as individuals.

How do spouses, relatives, or friends find the intestinal fortitude to stay in such a troubled relationship? Where does a child find the courage to love and repeatedly forgive an untreated AMAC parent who cannot be relied upon for basic stability, or for anything else? We don't know, but it brings tears to our eyes when we think about it during our recovery and afterward.

Do we FAMACs have a need to be needed? Are our lives so empty that we fear we might not find someone else who would have us? Perhaps we seek abuse because we too were mistreated as children and became perpetual victims seeking perpetual victimizers. It is not AAMAC's task to analyze the origins of such relationships, except as they relate to our own recovery. This issue belongs to the people involved with AMACs in some close relationship. The place to explore such questions is in private therapy for our families. Participation in the FAMAC workshops can facilitate and speed the private treatment, while private therapy enhances our efforts in the workshops.

The spouse of one member of our first AAMAC workshop has written about her family's life under his influence in the long years before his recovery began. Since she is still living with him now, she has written about the entire cycle of dysfunction and recovery:

LIVING WITH AN UNTREATED AMAC

Although I was not myself molested as a child, I am married to an AMAC, and the AAMAC book has enlightened me. I was seventeen years old and eight months pregnant when I married my husband. Shortly after our marriage, he began getting mad or irritated with me for no apparent reason. I just could not understand what was wrong with him. When I became angry, his behavior turned violent and destructive. He beat me and verbally abused me. Eventually, I learned to repress my anger and retreated into deep, solemn depressions. I am sure that, had we not had a dependent child, I would have ended my life during one of those horrible depressions.

I always felt that there was something lacking in me, something that I was not doing right which brought on my husband's erratic behavior. I knew that I was not pretty, nor very smart for that matter, and I did not really know how to act feminine or even to flirt. I thought that if I tried to be a good wife, mother, and homemaker, maybe then he might appreciate me. My effort did not help! Then I went to work, hoping that more money coming into our home would help. The little additional money was nice, but for some reason, he seemed to like me even less. I felt as though I was the last person he ever thought of. Sometimes he said nice things to me, only to take them away with a degrading and cruel remark a few hours later. I had grown up with very little confidence and self-esteem, and this marriage certainly didn't help, to put it mildly! Reading a book about child psychology, I realized that my husband must have had a bad childhood. I recalled that, not too long after we were married, he had begun exhibiting many of the behaviors described in the AAMAC book. I had also read other books on human behavior, and now things began to make sense to me. I remember trying to talk with him about how our childhood can affect our adult lives, but he was not responsive. I read self-help books for my own personal growth and well-being, and to understand my husband.

Eventually he and I began to talk together about our lives. This analysis helped until the facts of his molestation came out. Though I did not react in a negative way to this disclosure, he no longer would participate with me in the self-analytic exercises. I knew that he needed to talk more about having been molested as a child, but he would not discuss the matter further, and there was nowhere else for him to turn.

After that time, many years passed, and I felt like a failure. I knew that I had failed him, and so did he. He began to blame everything that happened on me. I accepted his brutal behavior because I felt that I had failed the one I loved. Things eventually got so bad that, because of excessive substance abuse, my husband ended up in a recovery program. I too joined a recovery program for the spouses. We have grown a great deal since then and our marriage has improved considerably. However, this issue of his childhood molestation was still a problem in both of our lives and the lives of our children.

My husband is now a member of Adults Anonymous Molested As Children. Believe me, the Program does work! I have seen my husband grow so much in a very short time. The AAMAC book has provided me with a good deal more knowledge about a subject that has until recently remained unknown. Through the Program, I have gained freedom from those false feelings of failure that I used to harbor. I can see now that I never could have helped my husband alone. He now is helping himself, as I too am helping myself. Together, we are growing closer by dealing with our own individual problems personally. We are happier than we have ever been through our many years together.

This wife of an AMAC expresses the pain of families in no uncertain terms. The heartache and trauma of an untreated AMAC affects the lives of people around them. Not all untreated AMACs act out their childhood traumas in the same ways, of course, but those we know and their spouses have certainly endured disrupted relationships. Since the whole family suffers from the erratic behavior of the AMAC, the entire family needs help to recover from the results. Without support, the dysfunctions are sure to continue, and the individuals may grow in different directions, with divorce and estrangement the unhappy result. Angry children grow up to become angry adults unless they see more objectively what has happened to them. Angry spouses continue to repress their hurt, doubts, fears, frustrations, resentments, and self-blame, unless they too acquire understanding. There is no one to blame, but only the cause and effect to grasp.

Yet many families ask, "Why should we have to be put through the ordeal of recovery when we did nothing wrong?" Recovery is not a punishment, but a matter of practical necessity. The spouse may not have suspected a troubled future when he married the untreated AMAC. The children were literally born into inherited problems.

"But why can't the AMAC get help and then everybody live happily ever after?" spouses say. "Therapy is so expensive, and we just can't afford it! This isn't fair!" Fair or not, nothing changes until intervention dislodges the dysfunctional patterns of the relationship. From the time of Job to the present day, sufferers have asked the despairing question, "Why me?" The answer may be simply, "Because of who we are." Who we are has a lot to do with where we find ourselves. We seldom reach a destination by mere accident. Complicated circumstances resulting from our choices led us to our condition in life. You are not reading this book by accident. You had to make some decisions and draw some conclusions from your life experience. You were seeking some answers, and the title of our book rang your chimes.

Is staying together worth a twice-monthly therapy session on the condition that everybody work on himself? We personally think it is cheaper to seek some type of therapy than to wait for divorce and the shattering of the family. The necessity that the whole family change may not seem fair, but without the support of family therapy, adjustment and reunification is very difficult, if not impossible, and ongoing maintenance will strengthen family relationships.

No matter what the original problem was, sooner or later, the responsibility of solving that problem rests with each person individually. Small children are the exception, of course, but once they reach the age of awareness they must also learn to work on their problems. All of this just goes along with growing up and learning how to improve what we can. Whatever applies to the AMAC in setting his life straight applies equally to the intimate circle around him.

It might be well to remember that the adult who was molested in childhood didn't have a choice in what happened to her either. That is no less fair. Everyone involved in an AMAC's life is a victim, including the AMAC. In order to accomplish recovery, each adult must take individual responsibility for his own life and share the responsibility for reaching the children and helping them to understand, grow, and recover harmony with the rest of the family.

In the words of John Donne, "no man is an island," complete in himself. Our individual lives affect the life of the whole social organism in which we participate and each other member of that organism—the family, the community, the state. If one family member is unfulfilled, the entire group can fall into disharmony. Given lengthy suffering under duress, standing alone, no one escapes. The problems of one member throw the whole family into crisis. By the same token, each member of the family and the family as a whole benefit from one member's choice to return to health.

Is it any wonder that we suggest therapy for the entire family of the AMAC? Our emotions and thoughts determine much of our behavior. We choose our response to events. We all feel basically the same emotions; what makes us unique is the way we express them. Our feelings and thoughts determine our behavior; we behave as we have learned to behave. If we learned a certain pattern, then it stands to reason that we can unlearn it. If we choose to solve our problems as we encounter them, we can lead more fulfilling lives. Other people who become involved with us will receive more satisfaction from the relationship, and they too can grow in a healthy way if they choose. How we react to each other determines what we become, healthy or not.

It makes sense, therefore, that the spouses of AMACs meet with each other once a week. They can discuss causes and effects in their personal lives, the actions and reactions that have interfered with their fulfillment as individuals and families. But there is still more. As we mentioned earlier, surely the AMAC played an important part in the family disharmony. He usually realizes this fact and accepts his responsibility. The spouse and older children of the AMAC, however, also participated in the family's breakdown. Blaming is hopeless at this stage. In FAMAC, the effort to reorganize the family in a healthier pattern can flourish. For one to be happy, all must grow toward happiness. Forgiveness is a great healer.

Once we forgive those who hurt us, we ourselves begin to heal. Understanding is the path to forgiveness. We have benefited from adding marriage, family, and child counseling to our workshop effort. Even if the family has separated and the spouses have divorced, the learned behaviors do not extinguish themselves. The children's problems, the spouse's repressed feelings, all continue to cause trouble in their future lives. We even advise divorced spouses to attend weekly FAMAC workshops and therapy, once these are established, to heal the devastation.

Keeping in mind that we are only as sick as we are secret, it is wise for us to rid ourselves of secrecy. The need comes to all of us to clean our psychological house, and now it is our turn. That may not feel fair, but these things happen anyway. We cannot change the world, but we can change ourselves. We can stop blaming and being angry. We are alive, and things happen. Right, wrong, blame—none of these concepts is constructive here. What matters is that something happened in our relationship, and we can find out what to do about it and try again.

It is not chance, but the way we live, that causes us pain. Our actions clash with the values we profess. We become irritable. We don't interact successfully with others, and we know it's time to change. We fear discovery of our inadequacy. The time to begin regaining some balance and growth is now. We have the opportunity to look clearly and honestly at ourselves. We want help. We have an emotional investment in the quest. Going on is more rewarding than escape. The causes of our grief are not simple, but we are responsible for our own conduct. We have Twelve Steps to follow and a book to guide us, along with meeting and working with others. The only question that remains is why haven't we started a FAMAC workshop and begun?

FOOTNOTE
The FAMAC program is just beginning. We invite the spouses of AAMAC members to help develop this society by establishing FAMAC workshops. Write to AAMAC WSO Inc., at P.O. Box 662, Apple Valley, CA 92307. If anyone wishes to share personal experiences, please send them to that same address, with permission to publish them anonymously. All material is subject to editing and revision. All material is nonreturnable and becomes the sole property of AAMAC WSO, Inc. Please write between thirty and fifty pages, preferably typed.

Although we may not be able to publish every personal experience, we are grateful for all contributions.

FAMAC TWELVE STEPS

Our FAMAC Twelve Steps are meant only as suggestions. The term "a power greater than ourselves" is a general term for God, the group, truth, therapy, or whatever we may know the power to be.

1. We admitted that we were powerless over what had happened to the AMAC, and that parts of our lives had become unmanageable.
2. Came to believe that a power greater than ourselves could help restore us to sanity.
3. Made a decision to share our will and our lives with a power greater than ourselves, keeping an open mind and accepting direction from those who are helping us.
4. Made a searching and fearless moral inventory of ourselves.
5. Admitted to ourselves and to another person the exact nature of our problems.
6. Were entirely ready to accept the help we need to reduce our short-comings and defects of character.
7. Humbly asked a power greater than ourselves to continue helping us in our recovery by giving us strength to work on our problems.
8. Made a list of all persons we had harmed and became willing to make amends to them.
9. Made direct amends wherever possible except when to do so would injure them or others.
10. Continued to take personal inventory and, when we were wrong, promptly admitted it.
11. Sought through prayer or meditation to improve our conscious con-tact with a power greater than ourselves, expecting only knowledge, direction, and the courage to heal.
12. Having improved as a result of working these Steps, we tried to carry this message to others, and to practice these principles in all of our affairs.

None among us has been able to maintain anything like perfect adherence to these principles. We are not saints. The point is that we are willing to improve. These steps are guides to progress. We claim progress rather than perfection. Those of us who practice these steps find that we have stronger purpose for recovery.

FAMAC TWELVE TRADITIONS

1. Our common welfare must come first. Personal recovery depends upon FAMAC unity.

2. For our purpose there is but one authority: a loving power greater than ourselves as expressed in our group conscience. Our leaders are but trusted servants. They do not govern.

3. The only requirements for membership are an age of eighteen or more and a desire to recover from the effects of having been somehow involved in a relationship with an adult who was molested as a child.

4. Each workshop is autonomous except in matters affecting other workshops or FAMAC as a whole.

5. Each workshop has the purpose to help ourselves recover and to carry our message to FAMACs who still suffer.

6. A FAMAC workshop ought never to endorse, finance or lend the FAMAC name to any related facility or outside enterprise lest problems of money, property and prestige divert us from our primary purpose.

7. Every workshop ought to be self-supporting, declining outside contributions.

8. FAMAC should remain forever nonprofessional, but our service centers may employ special workers.

9. FAMAC, as such, ought never to be organized, but we may create service boards directly responsible to those they serve.

10. FAMAC has no opinions on outside issues; hence our name ought never to be brought into public controversy.

11. Our public relations policy is based on attraction rather than promotion; we must always maintain the anonymity of other members and our AMAC counterparts.

12. Anonymity is the spiritual foundation of all our traditions, ever reminding us to place principles before personalities.

7

NEW BEGINNINGS

*Every human being discovers for himself the
meaning in his unique life. There is joy in
new beginnings, which give life new meaning.*

We are what we think. We base our choices upon our current state of
mind and awareness. If we are angry or depressed, then those feelings
color everything. Most AMACs see life in such a perspective, anticipat-
ing threats and interpreting events in pessimistic ways. With the help of
other AMACs, we can retrain our sight. We can choose how we see our
experience. If this were not so, we could never recover, for we couldn't
change our minds about anything.

In AAMAC, we are seeking new meaning in our lives, renegotiating
the relationship of our inner world with the material world to give ourselves the space to grow. In our relationships with other people, we find
our own true spiritual nature and allow others, if they choose, to find theirs.

We seek the truth for its own sake. Our new awareness washes away
the shame and stigma of our soiled yesterdays. The so-called secrets of
the universe are not secret at all. Though there is much wrong in the
world, for many of us recovering AMACs, much is right as well. Unless
we fix our sight on the whole picture, it is easy for us to avoid our most
important issues. That is always a serious error, regardless of our excuses.

Our problems originated in our fear of discovery and the effects of
that fear upon our adult lives. The spiritual energy we find in our
AAMAC society empowers us to walk in light through an inner life that
was formerly dark even to ourselves. With tolerance for the infinite vari-
eties of personal faith, we choose not to bicker about differences in religion and philosophy. We gather together to work instead on our
common problems, confident that mutual support will see us through.

We do feel the intense pain that characterizes an enlightenment acquired through self-discovery, pain from which no higher power can protect us. Nevertheless, none of us has regretted working on ourselves openly and honestly and facing ourselves head-on. If we were immune to pain, fear, and failure, we would not be in AAMAC. We would not have led our troubled lives. Our recovery is hard work, but pain is a messenger and a guide. It leads us into inner places from which we formerly excluded everyone, even ourselves. We do not want to silence that messenger. We want it to speak to us loud and clear because the sooner we arrive at the center of ourselves, the sooner we can heal. Alone, we might lack the fortitude to face and follow the road of anguish wherever it leads, but our friends and a power greater than ourselves support us on the healing journey. It sometimes seems easier to avoid the core issues that trouble us than to wrestle with them and resolve them. But our problems have affected our lives profoundly. We became so used to a dysfunctional way of thinking that we accepted it as necessary and persuaded ourselves that we were living fully. Because our childhoods were unhappy, we felt that all of life must be so. We were helpless then, but we certainly are not helpless now. We allowed the molester to continue governing our lives after we became adults and physically beyond his reach. We were not fools, but we certainly were naive, unfamiliar as we were with such wonders as a positive outlook on life.

Even after we overcome the fears of discovery, we must extinguish the pessimism that became habitual. We have difficulty declining to do what others ask, even if our cooperation damages our integrity. When someone makes an unfair request and we decline, we feel guilty. Most of us never really learned to say no. The perpetrator never took no for an answer. She manipulated us into submission.

Now we say no to the fear of discovery and yes to recovery. We say yes to the pursuit of joy and freedom. We say no to slickness and sickness. We are determined to reach our potential rather than be pawns for others to use in reaching theirs. AMACs who want the sweetest kind of revenge will find it in recovery, by insisting upon useful, happy lives despite our injuries.

Not all of the answers are in this book. In a few years, we will understand where we have been, though we cannot now anticipate where we will go. The real answers are living answers that evolve directly from interaction in AAMAC. These answers change and fluctuate according to our growth. In recovery, we constantly see old things in new ways. As our lives interweave and we share our experiences, the answers unfold and blossom into new beginnings. The little that we know as individuals expands in the collective consciousness of the workshop. We hope that others will experience the new freedom we have enjoyed in one another's company.

8 _____

WORKING THE TWELVE STEPS

At each new plane, we experience a new
state of infancy. Life is a journey of steps
from infancy to infancy.

Adults Anonymous Molested As Children is a Twelve Step Program. We have modified the original Twelve Steps of Alcoholics Anonymous to fit our particular needs. Working these AAMAC Twelve Steps enhances our lives and propels our recovery. They keep us oriented, centered, and conscious of the fact that we are here to learn how our childhood traumas have carried over into our adult lives.

Our Program works only for people who work it. If AAMAC is not helpful after a person has attended the workshops for a while, she may consider the distinction between being in the Program and working it. To be in AAMAC is merely to show up. To work the Program is to apply our Twelve Steps, and attend our AAMAC workshops to share experience, strength, and hope with other AMACs.

STEP ONE
WE ADMITTED THAT WE WERE POWERLESS OVER HAVING BEEN MOLESTED AS CHILDREN AND THAT PARTS OF OUR LIVES HAD BECOME UNMANAGEABLE.

Feelings of powerlessness are a hallmark of an AMAC's character. As adults, we express that powerlessness in two ways: as personalities who need to be cared for and as personalities who need not to be cared for. Most AMACs switch from one of these extremes to the other, although one usually dominates. We change without much warning, which often confuses the people closest to us.

We AMACs also carry the blame and guilt for having been molested as children, and we feel dirty as a result. By admitting that we were powerless over our molestation, we put down the burden of responsibility we have carried all our lives.

The second part of our First Step, admitting that parts of our lives had become unmanageable, speaks for itself. Most AMACs are only partially dysfunctional. We usually lead very problematic lives in those dysfunctional areas. We do not have to remain in a dysfunctional state, but can learn to be happier. To complete the work of this First Step, we identify which parts of our lives were unmanageable, a process which is not so simple as one may think. The workshop and the AAMAC Twelve Steps help us sort out the complexities and discover patterns in our behavior.

STEP TWO
CAME TO BELIEVE THAT A POWER GREATER THAN OURSELVES COULD HELP RESTORE US TO SANITY.

The phrase "a power greater than ourselves" is a general term for God, truth, the group, therapy, AAMAC, or whatever one understands it to mean. We are AMACs, and we do have sick egos. None of us showed up at the door of AAMAC already cured. No one who was molested as a child goes through life unscathed. Only with the help of a power greater than ourselves can our egos give way and cease obstructing the path to recovery. We must discover our dysfunctions and heal the insanity that breeds them. We cannot do that alone. If we could, we would not be here working these Twelve Steps. Admitting our childhood powerlessness, and the resulting unmanageability of our lives, humbles us. These admissions, however, also imply that we have alternatives, an idea which gives us hope at last.

The word sanity troubles some of us. Are we saying that we have been insane all these years? We must be honest with ourselves about this matter. We in AAMAC need not decide who is sane and who is not. We can only declare that we have led dysfunctional lives. Surely, we know the pain of our secrets. Would any sane person suffer this pain for so long and do nothing about it? Such trauma could indeed be termed insanity of sorts. We run the entire scale of human problems. Some of us are more traumatized than others. Whether mildly or severely troubled, however, we were not altogether mentally balanced. We must not deceive ourselves by glossing over our social and psychological condition and thereby miss our opportunity for recovery.

To be restored to sanity means to be restored to some reasonable balance and comfort. Beyond that, we leave terminology to each individual, who knows better than we. What matters is that we want to recover. We want a better way of life. If restoration to sanity is what it takes to bring us to this goal, then let it happen. We have nothing to fear for what we have been or for what happened to us as children. Let us all be honest with ourselves, make new beginnings, and get on with our healing together.

STEP THREE

MADE A DECISION TO SHARE OUR WILL AND OUR LIVES WITH A POWER GREATER THAN OURSELVES, KEEPING AN OPEN MIND AND ACCEPTING DIRECTION FROM THOSE WHO ARE HELPING US.

By now, we should have acquired enough information about ourselves to indicate, once and for all, that we need to take serious action. We have sought help in AAMAC. What other help do we need? Are we still fighting ourselves, people, places, and things? Are we sharing our experience, strength, and hope, and taking action on the results? Are we applying the direction we receive from AAMAC, our sponsors, our therapists? Are we keeping open minds about ourselves, others, and AAMAC as a whole?

We must obviously get out of our own way if we are to free ourselves from the bondage of our past, and to gain peace of mind. Seeking help, accepting direction, and keeping an open mind frees us to participate in our own recovery. Removing our attention from others and working our own Program gives us even greater freedom.

STEP FOUR

MADE A SEARCHING AND FEARLESS MORAL INVENTORY OF OURSELVES.

Here we are dealing with principles, standards, or habits, with respect to right or wrong conduct, ethics, and standards of sexual behavior. Now is the time to turn our attention from the perpetrator who blighted our lives and to focus upon ourselves. The AAMAC Twelve Steps continue to inform us, preparing us for this exercise and guiding us through it. We are opening the door to real freedom and lightening the burdens that we have dragged through our lives all these years.

Nobody says it is easy, but the task of facing ourselves is very rewarding. We list not only our faults but our strengths as well. We need to become familiar with our own goodness. All that we have done in the first three Steps should have prepared us for this Fourth Step. Thorough and unflinching honesty lets the cleansing sun shine upon our dark and musty secrets. Once we face them, they can no longer harm us.

STEP FIVE

ADMITTED TO OURSELVES AND TO ANOTHER PERSON THE EXACT NATURE OF OUR PROBLEMS.

Knowing these things about ourselves is one thing. It is obvious that we have always known, since we have always acted out our knowledge in symptomatic ways. What we most likely did not do was admit to ourselves, or to anybody else, what we knew about ourselves. Admitting our powerlessness in childhood; admitting the unmanageability of our lives; fostering hope; deciding to seek help; seeking that help and accepting direction; taking inventory—all of these efforts have led to a strong recovery.

Now what do we do with all this information? If, as we believe, we are only as sick as we are secret, then the answer is obvious. We give the knowledge away. Denial is an admission that something is wrong with us, an admission which is paradoxically wrapped in the insistence that nothing is wrong with us. We give up denial. Revealing to one other human being our knowledge of the worst about ourselves smashes the secrecy once and for all. We are on the true healing journey now, doing what no other can do for us: telling the truth about ourselves. The safest place to do that is with other AMACs whose own experience enables them to appreciate our vulnerability. Sharing the best and the worst of ourselves with another person is healing. The Fourth and Fifth Steps are essential milestones toward recovery.

STEP SIX

WERE ENTIRELY READY TO ACCEPT THE HELP WE NEED TO REDUCE OUR SHORTCOMINGS AND DEFECTS OF CHARACTER.

The Fourth and Fifth Steps usually turn up new information about ourselves that we need to deal with on a more concentrated level. We hope by now to have identified our troubles. This Step is a reaffirmation of the Second Step. Because we have been attending AAMAC and working on ourselves for a while, we may slack off now and fail to follow through. We may deceive ourselves with the belief that we can do the rest on our own. Knowing what we now know about ourselves and about others can leave us vulnerable to many types of harm. We are wide open, and we do not want to hurt ourselves or others either by exposing ourselves to risk or defending too rigidly against it. Just as we would not attempt to do heart surgery on ourselves and close our own wounds, we must not attempt to do psychic surgery and close those wounds without aid. This is not the time to show our independence.

STEP SEVEN

HUMBLY ASKED A POWER GREATER THAN OURSELVES TO CONTINUE HELPING US IN OUR RECOVERY BY GIVING US STRENGTH TO WORK ON OUR PROBLEMS.

This Step is a reaffirmation of the Third Step. It is definitely an active exercise. Again, we are not doctors. We are not knowledgeable enough to heal ourselves alone. Even therapists seek the help of other therapists, and doctors need the medical treatment of other doctors. We must be equally humble and find the help we need for a complete recovery. Half measures can bring only half results. We need to be thorough now, while we have the chance and are open to change. If we undergo this process now, we can be done with it. We have known pain enough. Now is the time to tie up the loose ends and change the things we can.

STEP EIGHT

MADE A LIST OF ALL PERSONS WE HAD HARMED AND BECAME WILLING TO MAKE AMENDS TO THEM.

The Eighth Step rattles an AMAC's inner being. We are self-justifiers and blamers. We have carried our secrets for years. We have tried to act as if everything were all right. We carried overwhelming feelings of betrayal, abandonment, guilt, and fear. Nobody who feels such emotions is tossing flowers and kisses to the world. We need to work this Step and get it over with. There is no skating around our own actions.

We may complicate matters with vengefulness, thinking, "I did this because he did that, and I therefore don't owe him any amends." Such justification obstructs our recovery. When we harm others, we harm ourselves. The harm has the effect of species hatred which circles back upon ourselves. If we are not willing to deal with these facts, then we cannot clear the wreckage of our past.

STEP NINE

MADE DIRECT AMENDS TO SUCH PEOPLE WHEREVER POSSIBLE, EXCEPT WHEN TO DO SO WOULD INJURE THEM OR OTHERS.

We AMACs can be clever, outsmarting ourselves in this Step. Again, self-honesty and sincerity are the key. We are working these Steps for ourselves. One result is a developing sense of empathy and compassion for ourselves to replace the loathing, pity, and low self-esteem. We must also develop a sense of empathy and compassion for others. When we speak of making direct amends wherever possible, we mean to be practical. We needn't crawl twenty miles on hands and knees over broken glass and kiss somebody's rear end through a screen door in order to call it amends. We approach others with sincerity and purpose and we lay our cards on the table.

It is wise to begin with making amends to ourselves for the harm we have done. If we have diligently worked the previous eight Steps, we should already have a pretty good idea about the ways we have injured ourselves. Then we can turn to the people closest to us, our spouses, children, brothers, sisters, parents, grandparents, and close friends.

The question often arises whether we owe our perpetrator any kind of amends. Not surprisingly, most AMACs answer an emphatic NO! The subject makes for good debate. Perhaps the perpetrator has tried to make amends to us, and we rejected his efforts. Perhaps he was a drug addict or alcoholic and has since turned his life around and sincerely regrets his transgressions against us. Perhaps he even found out that he was an AMAC and is working the AAMAC Program, trying to set his life straight. Should he try to make restitution to us and we attack him, do we then owe him amends? It is up to each of us as individuals to answer such questions. There is not one cut-and-dried answer.

Others we have harmed are more distant; we may have lost contact with them, or they may even have died. Our Eighth Step requests only that we show good faith and willingness to make amends to them all.

The condition, "except when to do so would injure them or others," is not an excuse to avoid making amends, but a suggestion to construct better relationships with other people, and, if that be impossible, at least to acknowledge the wrongs to another person such as a sponsor. If a woman has had an affair with a married man, for instance, it may not be wise to apologize to his wife, especially if she is still married to the man and unaware of his actions. We wish to clear away debris, not to create new problems for ourselves and others.

We needn't confess our moral inventory as a part of our amends. Good judgment, honesty, and sincerity are essential elements of Step Nine. Whenever possible, it is advisable to be brief and restrain the impulse to review wrongdoing by the persons we injured. Our aim is to relieve the burden of the pain we have caused in their lives, not to extract retribution from them. This matter is not their problem, but ours.

If making amends to a family member would expose the perpetrator, we must use our own judgment. Most of us do not protect perpetrators. We confront them, regardless of who they are or what the circumstances. If making amends exposes the perpetrator and that causes problems in the family, we feel the perpetrator can deal with it.

Steps Ten, Eleven, and Twelve are what we call our Maintenance Steps. The first nine Steps walk us through the deluge and wreckage of our past. They guide us into recovery by leading us one step at a time through our insanity or dysfunctions, with some clarity and comfort. They provide us with hope and tools and reward us for our efforts. The AAMAC Maintenance Steps continue the process of recovery. They help us to continue processing all the information we have acquired and the results of our new insight in our daily lives. The first nine Steps linked the past with the present. The Maintenance Steps bridge the past and the future. Each of us uses them in ways uniquely our own. These Twelve Steps are not laws or weapons for judging others, but only guides to progress.

STEP TEN

CONTINUED TO TAKE PERSONAL INVENTORY AND, WHEN WE WERE WRONG, PROMPTLY ADMITTED IT.

Regrets are old and mostly useless memories. In our present stage of recovery, would we do the same things again that we did in the past? Can we unexperience that past and all that happened in consequence? Can we unsay the harmful words or take back the pain our words and deeds caused others? Now that we know the facts, it is time to put the past behind us and concentrate on building a healthy future. We can do this by becoming alert to our present circumstances and our responses to them. We continue attending AAMAC workshops, being honest with ourselves and others in our current stage of recovery, and catching ourselves in our errors. We admit the mistakes we make so we can learn to live in healthier ways. Knowing that we can never be perfect, we accept our best effort and credit ourselves with the progress we have made, despite our human frailties.

STEP ELEVEN

SOUGHT THROUGH PRAYER OR MEDITATION TO IMPROVE OUR CONSCIOUS CONTACT WITH A POWER GREATER THAN OURSELVES, EXPECTING ONLY KNOWLEDGE, DIRECTION, AND THE COURAGE TO HEAL.

If we are to stay in the mainstream of our recovery, we cannot afford an ego trip to clutter our path. We must continue healthy maintenance of both our spiritual and mental condition. We must have an energy source from which we can continue to charge ourselves up when our emotional batteries begin to run down. We must be able to trust in this energy source for the nurturing and power that we need to continue in our recovery. We can benefit from that source only by improving on its uses and striving to understand it better. Whether we take comfort from prayer, meditation, group activity, or other means, we cannot recover by and of ourselves. We would not be here in AAMAC workshops and working the Twelve Step Program if we could have done better by ourselves. We needed a power greater than ourselves and we sought out AAMAC. A power greater than ourselves, like life, has the meaning we give it. We must believe and trust in it. If we are to keep it, we must maintain contact with it and exercise the knowledge, direction, and the power to carry that out. It is prayer, meditation, or some other energizing type of activity which gives us access to that power.

STEP TWELVE

HAVING IMPROVED AS A RESULT OF WORKING THESE STEPS, WE TRIED TO CARRY THIS MESSAGE TO OTHERS WHO WERE MOLESTED AS CHILDREN, AND TO PRACTICE THESE PRINCIPLES IN ALL OF OUR AFFAIRS.

We are willing to grow. The principles of these Steps are guides to progress. We claim progress rather than perfection. What better way to continue progress along the path of recovery than to work with others? Our fellowship exists only because the first members of AAMAC carried the message to other people. Service benefits us as much as it does those we serve. It permits us to expand our horizons beyond our personal limits, to clarify our understanding of what we are about, and to feel the nurturing power of our own health. Our new members constantly infuse AAMAC with their unique insight, which inspires all of us, new members and old.

9

HELPING OTHERS

Lost child, trapped in an adult body, if you
are reaching out, then reach out to me.
I will be there.

It is important to our own recovery that we reach out to others and give them what was given so freely to us. Other AMACs helped bring us to our present point of recovery. To love, one must give. To remain healthy and active, one must serve others.

The path we recommend is mapped out in the principles of the AAMAC Program; our AAMAC Twelve Steps and Traditions along with other AAMAC literature; and regular participation in at least one AAMAC workshop each week. We don't ask that anybody like this process, but we know that it is one road to recovery. If we work the AAMAC Program, then the Program works for us. Doing so requires less effort than keeping our heads above water while remaining dysfunctional. We are not an emotional welfare program, but more like a stock exchange: a minimal investment brings minimal returns. Recovery requires hard work. There are, however, no bad investments in AAMAC.

We must attend AAMAC workshops with the right attitude, which is nothing more than a helping attitude. Even if we are upset and angry, we can develop a helping attitude as a tool to propel us from selfishness. Everything we do in AAMAC transfers back to our own personal lives and relationships.

Helping others begins with helping ourselves. AAMAC workshops are support groups, not attack groups. It is not our purpose to extract information from one another; we seek only to exchange information about ourselves. We guard against crosstalk, which can get out of hand and turn into confrontation without warning.

AMACs can remember only so much at a time. Many of our memories make us uncomfortable. Until we are at ease knowing what we know about ourselves, we should not have to be coerced by confrontation. Instead, we should support each other with true caring, authenticity, empathy, warmth, and respect.

Sponsoring other AMACs is a very important function of workshop members, but some of us need more time than others to heal. The length of our time in AAMAC should not be the primary criterion for merit as a Sponsor. Since we cannot give away what we do not have, a prospective Sponsor must be honest with herself about her motives. If she feels that she remains dysfunctional in major areas of her life, she can decline a request to act as a colleague's Sponsor.

A person who is still significantly dysfunctional should wait to sponsor another member, in order to avoid sharing dysfunctions rather than recovery. That would retard another AMAC's progress rather than enhance it. At the same time, we remember that nobody has ever been able to recover perfectly, in this Program or any other. We all relapse periodically into former behavior. We must not be so critical of ourselves that we fail to give away what we could share. If one is honest and reasonably comfortable with his overall life and recovery, then chances are that he will be a helpful Sponsor.

Sponsors are not marriage counselors, psychotherapists, judges, attorneys, or juries. An adequate number of professionals are already doing that fine work. Nor are Sponsors divinely appointed guardians gifted with divine wisdom. We are all trying to get better rather than be cured. Sponsors are not surrogate parents, either, and those whom they sponsor are not children. A sponsorship is a trusting and helping adult relationship, one AMAC helping another AMAC. We are quite set in our ways as adults and AMACs. We establish our Program on suggestions, not insistence. Taking pain as the great teacher, we listen to our Sponsor's suggestions, but we decide for ourselves.

A good Sponsor uses the AAMAC Program as the primary guide. We do not allow outside literature to be sold under the AAMAC symbol, nor do we distribute it at our workshops, lest we divert ourselves from our primary purpose. AMACs who seek sponsorship are looking for help with the AAMAC Program, not some other process. Although valuable outside information can also help us, we focus our attention on practicing AAMAC principles in all our affairs. One does not go to a Jewish synagogue to practice Catholicism or enroll in a school of sociology to study engineering. We attend AAMAC to follow that Program, which we know works.

A Sponsor never dictates the solution to a problem, but only suggests alternatives, leaving the final choices to the person she is sponsoring. Certain questions help the Sponsor to stay on track: Is the person we sponsor attending AAMAC workshops regularly, working the Twelve Steps, comprehending the AAMAC literature, and working with others? Is she trying to rewrite our program to fit her dysfunctions, or is she honestly facing herself, trying to recover? Is she changing her behavior or persisting in old strategies? Is she trying to set us up to take the blame for her living problems? Does she need outside professional help, and is she willing to seek it? Are we allowing her to waste our time? Are we wasting her time by listening more about other people's problems rather than her own, and not centering her on herself? Are we straightforward and honest with her? Is she straightforward and honest with us? Are we helping her to heal, or enabling her dysfunctional behavior? Is she abusing drugs or alcohol and crying on our shoulder while under the influence?

These questions help protect us from being abused and getting in over our heads. If those we sponsor flagrantly disregard our suggestions and continue in their dysfunctional living patterns, then obviously they do not want what we have. We cannot change them. We can help them only if they allow us to do so. Being a Sponsor does not require us to let someone wipe his feet on us. We must be firm, but not unfair. The best and safest way to sponsor someone in AAMAC is to use the AAMAC Program as our primary guide to progress. We already know that our Program works because we have worked it ourselves.

Sponsorship is not something to be taken lightly, but a privileged role. When someone asks us to serve as Sponsor, he sees some recovery in us that he wants for himself. Is what he sees in us authentic? Have we truly recovered to the extent he thinks? Probably not. We all fall short of others' expectations of us. But we have been in AAMAC for a while, and we have acquired a good deal of knowledge; we usually have more understanding of ourselves and one another than we once did. We are practiced in the AAMAC Program. People new to AAMAC are usually disillusioned before they meet us. They may be easily impressed and influenced by the way we present ourselves as long-time members. We must therefore be careful to be honest with them and tell the truth about ourselves. Trust, truth, confidentiality, and an open mind are indispensable.

Is our own house reasonably in order? How are we still dysfunctional? Can we be objective about those we sponsor? How well do we know AAMAC practices, principles, and objectives? How well do we apply the Program in our own lives? Can we be honest about our character defects and shortcomings when we are sharing with those whom we sponsor? If we are going to share our personal AAMAC Program of recovery, it is important that we have a Program to share. None of us is applying for sainthood. All of us could improve ourselves.

People from other Twelve Step Programs who come to us in order to deal specifically with AMAC problems can be a great asset, but their other Program may be crucial to their overall well-being and survival. Never do we suggest that our Program is better.

We never present Adults Anonymous Molested As Children as a cure-all or claim superiority to other Twelve Step groups. We never tell AMACs working another Twelve Step Program that we are the psychological pot of gold at the end of their emotional rainbow or, for that matter, anybody else's. Nothing could be further from the truth. Our Program is only as good as those who work it. We are only a path for AMACs to follow through their problems into something better, and to maintain their current level of recovery. We only wish to serve. Alcoholics' and addicts' abandonment of their Twelve Step Program could cause their death. Should they intend to switch groups instead of adding AAMAC to complement their other Programs, we advise them not to do it. We can be some things to all AMACS, but we cannot be all things to all AMACs. We can enhance anyone's overall recovery, but we are not an answer for problems other than AMACism.

Any AMAC member seeking a Sponsor would be wise to exercise caution. When an uncomfortable situation with a Sponsor arises, we first discuss the matter. If the difficulty cannot be resolved, we discontinue the relationship immediately. Sponsorship is an extra benefit of the AAMAC Program, but lacking a good match, it is better to use other sources. The AAMAC workshop as a whole can function as Sponsor. A few close friends in the Program could group and exchange information confidentially. Some AMACs prefer to use their therapists as primary Sponsors. An AAMAC Sponsor is not essential to recovery. Sponsors are only as good as the Program they are working for themselves.

2

PERSONAL EXPERIENCES

These personal experiences are candid and explicit. They are written by AMACs for AMACs, not for entertainment purposes. The details enable us to identify ourselves in our own minds and to show other AMACs that our secrets can be overcome. People who are offended by strong language and harsh events may be uncomfortable reading the following pages.

10

JUST LOVE ME

For as long as I can remember, abuse has been a big part of my life. I have been abused mentally as well as sexually. The mental abuse began when I was about six years old and continued until I was nineteen or twenty years old. In school, I was the main attraction; everybody loved to make fun of me. I felt that the highlight of my classmates' life would be to drive me to insanity or the brink of suicide.

I was so miserable that I often did consider suicide. I could see no other way to end my pain and suffering. I still think about it today, but not as much as I used to. When I first entered junior high school, my suffering only got worse. I used to lie in bed at night and fantasize about my own funeral. I hoped that I would go to sleep at night and never wake up.

It was very painful for me to listen to my few girlfriends talk about their boyfriends. Most guys just ran the other way when they saw me coming. I used to smile and pretend I knew what the other girls were talking about, but inside I was crying, and my heart was breaking. It probably wouldn't have hurt so much if I had received some support and understanding at home. Instead, my dad mentally abused me, and my mother overprotected me. I feel a lot of anger toward my parents. They have hurt me a great deal in many ways. During my youth, I didn't have any place or person to turn to for relief.

Music was and still is my escape from life and daily problems. While I was growing up, I withdrew into myself, my own little world. I didn't like reality. It was cruel, mean, and ugly. So when I wasn't crying myself to sleep, I was listening to music and singing. I sang about the things that I knew and felt in my heart. I felt that I could never have happiness, love, friends, and peace of mind. But even if I couldn't actually have these pleasures, I felt that I could imagine them through dreams and singing. As I grew older, my love for music increased. The more I sang about the things I longed for, the better singer I became. Now I sing because I enjoy it and music has helped keep me sane.

I craved affection and love, and the price didn't seem to matter at the time. Children who don't receive love search for it and get it from anyone and in any way they can find. At the age of thirteen I was sexually molested by a man who managed a furniture store. He was very nice to me, which is what I so badly wanted. He told me that he wanted to show me some furniture in the back room, where he began to fondle my breasts. Then he asked to kiss my breasts. I told him that I had to go, and he didn't try to stop me.

When I told my parents about the molestation, they started yelling at me! They reported the incident to the police, and after I took a lie detector test, the perpetrator admitted that he had molested me. The judge put him on probation, sentenced him to counseling, and that was the end of it. He didn't spend one day in jail—not one day! They let him go, and there is no telling how many children he has molested since.

Although the man who molested me received counseling, there was no help for me. We have what we call the criminal justice system, and that's exactly what it is: justice for the criminal and injustice for the victim. Nobody ever mentioned my experience again. My family didn't talk about such dirty things as that. They were just swept under the carpet and forgotten as though they had never happened. It all made me feel very dirty.

I'm sure that, if things had continued the same, I would be lying in the cemetery now, but I moved to another state in 1979. Now my life wasn't terrific, but it did change for the better. I had more friends, and some of them were men. Of course, I still didn't have a boyfriend, but at least I didn't run men out of the room.

When my high school English class voted me president, I was in shock for a week. In gym, I was no longer the last one to be chosen for a team. In fact, once, the captain chose me among the first. Finally, even with a learning disability nobody knew about, I graduated from high school. I had, by this time, buried the molestation deep inside.

I went to college to become a special education aide, and also did volunteer work for three years with special children. I gave them love and acceptance that I had never received. While I was in college, my learning disability was identified; to put it simply, I don't understand what I read. I asked for tutoring because of some trouble I was having with my classwork, but I saw my tutor only once because he started coming on to me sexually. When he touched me, something snapped. I can't remember ever having experienced the fear that I felt at that moment.

I became really confused. Since that experience, I have been afraid of men. If they touch me in any way, I go to pieces. Earlier in my life, I had always frightened people because of the way I looked. Nobody had ever wanted to look at me. Now a man was making sexual advances toward me of his own free will. It blew my mind.

In college, I began to see people differently than I had. They no longer acted as if I were a freak. I was used to playing the part of the punching bag. Now nobody threw any punches anymore. They actually treated me like a human being, and I couldn't handle it. I fixed that. If no one would satisfy my addiction to low self-esteem, then I would take over and abuse myself.

Besides shaking to death when a man smiled at me, I thought that he was either blind, crazy, or both. I couldn't see how anyone could love me because I felt, and still do, so much hate toward myself. I also have trouble trusting people, especially men, and I'm afraid to let people get close to me; I'm still afraid of eventual rejection. I am also addicted to old emotions, behaviors, and attitudes, especially to rejection. It's ironic that I should be hooked on the thing I fear most.

I really want love and affection. Now I know that such affirmations are unfamiliar to me and consequently felt alien to me whenever I encountered them. So I rejected the very love and affection I yearned for. When someone offers me love, I run and hide like a scared little girl. I feel that, if I let someone love me, I'll become addicted to his love and be devastated when he rejects me. I still elicit rejection because acceptance feels so strange. I do this mostly with men. If I can get them to hurt or reject me, then I can prove to myself that men are dirt, just as I thought. Understanding how this process works is a high point in my growth. I'm working to overcome these responses, and I can feel myself growing and changing.

I have never had a loving relationship with a man. I have had a few brief encounters, but, when the men found out they couldn't have their way with me fast enough, they hit the road. I felt that sex was all they had in mind. I didn't feel that they really cared for me—all they wanted was my body. And that's another thing—I'm so ashamed of my body that I can't see how a man could find me attractive. To each his own, I guess.

Sometimes I feel the only way to get a man to love me is to unbutton my shirt, let him fondle me, and have sex with him.

This whole experience has really been hard. On one hand, I feel all this anger and fear. On the other, I am very lonely. I want someone I love to love me just because I am me. I want to be held, touched, and cuddled. I have never been touched by a man in a soft and caring way. Part of my problem is that I am only willing to go so far. If a guy starts talking about going all the way, I run. I know that it's not possible for me to have an adult relationship without some sexual involvement, but sex scares me. So I accept that I will never be able to have the kind of relationship I want while I feel the way I do right now. I want the love, caring, and friendship, but sex just turns my stomach. Every time I see a couple holding hands, I turn and look the other way because it breaks my heart.

I am feeling progressively better now. I know that I am not cured, by any means, but I am better. At present, I am dealing with my anger toward men. I still have fears about being accepted, but I'm nowhere near as troubled as I was three years ago. I refuse to regress. I now have male friends who love and accept me as I am. I now demand that I get my hugs from everyone in my AAMAC group, men included. I'm proud to say that I enjoy these hugs. I know that some day I will be free from my self-imposed bondage. I am a recovering adult who was molested as a child, and I am recovering. The fact of my recovery is beautiful.

11

PATHWAY FROM HELL

My parents were alcoholics, and we were poor. I was taught very early in life not to feel, not to talk, and not to trust. My parents told me things like, "Do as I say, not as I do. Stand on your own two feet. Never ask anyone for help. Don't ever start trouble, but don't ever run from it either. Don't play with yourself or with anyone else because it is dirty and nasty. If you touch your penis for any reason other than going to the bathroom, it will fall off, and you will die."

My parents used to tease my brothers and me. They always ridiculed us if we made a mistake. Their behavior toward us was unpredictable, especially when they drank. I often woke up to cussing and screaming, and to sounds of breaking furniture and flesh hitting flesh. The black eyes, split lips, scratches, and bruises on my parents' bodies were unbelievable. My two brothers and I tried to stop our parents from beating each other while they were in drunken rages, only to be beaten ourselves. Anyone who has been through it surely understands the pain of living in that never-ending cycle of the alcoholic environment.

I am going to share secrets with readers of this book which I swore I would never tell another soul. These deep hidden secrets almost destroyed me. Each time they surfaced, they brought me great pain, anger, unexplainable behaviors, and overpowering fear. I used to think that I was the only one who had such secrets. I was afraid of anyone's ever discovering them. I feared that, if anyone found out the truth about me, I would be unwanted, unloved, and rejected. This was, to say the least, a painful way to live. Now I have nothing to hide. Sharing my secrets with other people helps me to feel better inside.

My first sexual experiences happened when I was five years old. My twelve-year-old cousin called me on the phone and invited me to come over to her house and listen to records. After I arrived, we went down into the basement, roller skated, and listened to rock 'n' roll. My cousin asked me to play house. I recall that she had a strange look in her eyes.

I accepted her invitation, and we went over to a double bed in a corner of the basement. She asked me whether I knew where babies came from and how they were made. I thought a stork brought them. I still believed in Santa Claus, elves, and the Easter Bunny. When she told me that these creatures didn't exist, I felt angry and upset. I felt that people I had trusted had lied to me.

My cousin held me close to her because I was crying. There was a big difference, she told me, between boys and girls, men and women. She touched me between my legs. It felt good, but I was afraid because of what my parents had taught me about sex, that it was dirty and sinful. I was afraid that my penis would fall off if I continued letting my cousin fondle me. I pulled away, and she asked me what was wrong. When I told her, she laughed and said I was stupid; those were lies I had been told to scare me. She assured me that mommies and daddies did these things all the time and that I had nothing to fear. I was still afraid someone might catch us. What would happen to me? What would God do to me? What would other people think of me? Would I be locked up for the rest of my life? Desire won out and overpowered all my fears, but not my guilt.

When I saw my cousin nude, I was shocked because she was different from me. I thought her penis had fallen off because she had played with herself. She told me to lie down, and she sucked me. When she was done, she told me to do it to her. I soon discovered that I enjoyed this sexual play. I remember that when she climaxed, I thought she had died as she fell on top of me. We made a vow never to tell anyone. This would be our secret forever. If I told, she would say I had raped her, and nobody would believe me. They would lock me up for the rest of my life. After that first time, I couldn't wait to be with her and repeat our "secrets."

Eventually, this cousin told another of my cousins about one of our secrets. When I found out, I felt betrayed. It turned out that they both wanted sex with me. They did everything they could think of with me. I also got excited watching them have oral sex with one another. Eventually, they asked me to join them in this activity. My two brothers walked in while we were doing our thing. I was horrified. They just laughed and took off their clothes. As I watched in bewilderment, each brother took one of my cousins and did everything that I had been doing all week! I felt hurt, betrayed, angry, and humiliated. They threatened that, if I told anybody what we had done, they would curse me, and I would die a slow, painful death. Besides, no one would believe me anyway. My cousins and I never had sex again. My brothers and I never spoke about the interlude. I gradually withdrew, building walls around me so no one could hurt me again.

When I was six, my thirteen-year-old uncle took me camping. We built a fire and drank some whiskey that he had stolen. My uncle told me that he would keep the fire going all night to protect me from the wild animals if I would do as he said. He scared the hell out of me. I remember seeing an expression on his face and in his eyes similar to the one I first saw on my cousin's face. Before bed, he encouraged me to have a few more drinks of whiskey. After that, my head began to spin. He gave me a hug, and I felt safe as I hugged him back. Suddenly, he pushed me backwards and pulled off my shorts. I was terrified as I saw his head go to my groin. When he finished with me, he stood up, grabbed me by my hair, and pulled my head to his crotch. As I tried to pull away, he began hitting me and yelling at me. He told me to suck him, threatening to let the ghosts get me if I refused. He made me masturbate him until he exploded in my mouth. I bit him. Then he beat me with his fists while calling me a bitch and a whore.

Still hitting me and screaming, he threw me onto my stomach. I felt his rough hands pull my buttocks apart. I was screaming, kicking, and crying. I tried to get away all the time he was hurting me. Suddenly, I screamed and could not breathe because of the burning pain of his penis being forced into my anus. It actually ripped me apart! He rammed it deep inside me while he continued to beat me. I screamed and begged him to stop, but he persisted for what seemed like hours. After he had finished, he made me lick him clean. I still remember the smell and taste of my own stool, blood, and his semen. He kept me tied up for the next two days and nights, letting me loose only to rape me.

I was powerless. I felt hopeless and useless. I reached a point during that camping trip where I no longer cared what happened to me, what I was doing, or when I did it. These brutal rapes continued through the next six years of my life. Wherever and whenever my uncle and I were alone, I submitted to his commands. Besides threatening to beat and kill me if I revealed what he had done to me, he said that other kids would call me names and reject me if they found out. If my family knew about his attacks, they would disown me and lock me up forever. Besides, who would believe me anyway?

By the time I was twelve, I hated everyone and everything. I withdrew deeper into myself. I was a loner and a rebel. I felt so different, as though I wasn't as good as everyone else. I felt undeserving of whatever good things happened to me. Other people hadn't done the dirty, nasty, sinful things I had. I knew that no one would ever understand the feelings of pain, remorse, fear, guilt, and anger I was carrying around inside me. My whole attitude was to shut off my feelings and live behind a mask, trusting no one.

Other children had family pleasures with their parents. Other children seemed to enjoy life and have a lot of fun. But I lost my childhood. My grades dropped. I wouldn't study. I disrupted my classes and got into other kinds of trouble. I was doing things my way and rebelling against everything. I wanted attention, and I got it by getting into trouble. I repeated sixth grade and became a tough guy. I started drinking heavily.

Eventually my dad sold his business. We moved to a small town and rented an apartment. My parents were planning to start a new life, and I was not included in their plans. To make things worse, I told them what my uncle had been doing to me for years, and they got mad at me. They called me a liar and told me such things didn't happen in our family. Then they made me swear not to tell anyone and threatened harm if I should.

One Christmas my brother brought a friend home for the holidays. They were stationed in the navy together. I was now thirteen. I saw the same look in the friend's eyes that I had seen in my cousins' and uncle's. It was as if they had a desire for me from their soul. One night my brother's friend woke me up stroking my penis. I was so frozen with fear I couldn't speak or move. He sucked me and then asked me if I liked it. I just nodded. Then he did it again until I climaxed. Old memories of my uncle flashed through my mind. He told me that if I said anything, I would regret it the rest of my life. These molestations continued for the next three nights. I had to climax before he would leave me alone. I wanted to die!

After my family moved, my life got worse. I was a loner, and I began running with gangs and using drugs. All I really wanted was to fit in somewhere. I wanted to belong to something, but I was so afraid, I couldn't allow anyone to get close to me. I was hiding from my real feelings, never wanting anyone to discover what I thought, who I was, or what I was carrying around inside. I was in a bad way, and things were getting worse.

I met a girl who reminded me of my first cousin. I got involved with her, but when I became sexual with her, she rejected me. I was hurt, and I took revenge by having sex with three of her girlfriends. I was very confused over which sex I preferred. I didn't want guys, yet I felt I didn't deserve girls. After all, if girls knew how dirty I was because of my past, they wouldn't want anything to do with me. That was when I made the decision to bury my secrets in the back of my mind and take them to my grave with me. I also vowed never to have sex with another male for the rest of my life. I felt that they would only use me for their own selfish satisfaction. My fear of physical abuse was overpowering.

In the mid-sixties, I met the girl who is now my wife. I got her pregnant, and we married at seventeen. We had a boy and, twenty months later, a girl. I played around on my wife before and after we were married. During our first four years together, we moved from place to place. My drinking and drug abuse increased, and so did our problems. I was searching for some new and exciting experiences, still trying to fill some void inside me. I had to be in control of everyone and everything. I had to show people that I was cool and could handle life. Suppressing my feelings of inadequacy only caused me to take out my rage on those closest to me. I expected my wife and family to cover up my behavior. I grew more like my parents as time went on, especially when I drank and used drugs.

I had affairs with nine other women during my nineteen years of marriage. I became the very things I did not want to be. I beat my wife and children. My wife didn't understand me because I never told her what was going on inside me. I was afraid of her rejection; if she knew, I might lose her, and I didn't want that to happen. I was also hiding two homosexual affairs that I became involved in during our marriage. After those two experiences, I reached an even lower state of mind. It all just added more shame and guilt to my life, which I carried for the next thirteen years.

With every form of self-deception, I tried to prove that I could get better on my own and still keep my secrets. I almost went insane. I would rather have died than tell you the truth about myself. I tried religion, self-help books, and psychiatrists, all the while hoping that someday I would just forget all that had ever happened to me. Sooner or later, everything I tried turned to failure.

Then I met the people in AAMAC, who understood what was going on with my life. They knew why I ran in fear to hide my secrets. They had been in those kinds of rages which caused them to be locked up. They were familiar with rejection by families and friends because of their uncontrollable behavior. They knew what it felt like to blame the world and retreat into isolation rather than face their problems. They also knew that many of these problems came directly from their having been molested as children. No more secrets. THEY KNEW!

In joining them, I have found a way out. I now know in my heart that all the things that happened to me as a child were not my fault; they never have to happen again. Not only have I found people who understand me, but they too are finding a way out of the wilderness. They want and need me as much as I want and need them.

I had to make my own decision. I ripped off the mask and opened my mind. I got honest with myself and became willing to look at the truth about myself. I share my feelings with one other person, and I no longer hide my secrets. This person, another adult who was molested as a child, is now my sponsor and friend. He does not judge me for what happened in my life. He cares enough about me to be truthful about his own life. He understands my behavior and relates personally to the destructive acts that I have committed. I know a new freedom that I never felt before. For years, my past had been destroying me and hindering my happiness. Today, my life is better, though still uncomfortable at times. I desire now to go forward and not to be tied down in the hellish prison of my past! I no longer have to make excuses for what I've done. Living in truth does set me free.

There are twelve simple Steps to work, and I try to follow them every day. They help me not to dwell on the horrors of my past or worry about the future. Today, I do have peace in my life. I share my secrets with my wife and have no fear of her rejecting me. She has forgiven me for all the cruel things I have done to her through the years. Our sharing has helped us make a better life together. I now want to be there for others who suffered as I have suffered. I want to walk with them down that road to a happier, healthier way of life. Freedom from my past, the knowledge that I never have to fear it again, releases me to enjoy living today.

If you are an adult who was molested as a child, you no longer have to hide the secrets or be alone again. Someday maybe we can help you to help yourself. Our doors and our hearts are open and waiting for you. We will be here. Don't wait long. The secrets can and will destroy you as they almost destroyed me.

12

MY LIFE AS I SEE IT TODAY

I cannot remember much of my life, but have blocked out memory as a way of dealing with a painful childhood. During the past six months of therapy, my views of my childhood have already changed. I am far from being recovered, but I look forward to the day when my past no longer haunts or mystifies me.

I do remember that my mother was a domineering person who needed to have control over everything. Although she had four kids in three and a half years, she prides herself on never having had two babies in diapers or on the bottle at the same time. I am the second oldest and the only girl. In therapy I discovered that a babysitter named Johnny molested me when I was four years old. My brothers and I slept upstairs in one big room. After Johnny put us to bed, he always went to the door and turned out the lights. He closed the door to make it appear that he had left the room. Then he crawled on his hands and knees under the window so my brothers wouldn't see his shadow. When he got to my bed, he fondled me. I don't remember what he told me to prevent my telling anyone, but I never told!

Once either Johnny or his brother took me into a woodshed while we were playing hide-and-seek. He pulled down his pants to show me his private parts. (I wasn't impressed; I had three brothers.) That's all I remember about the incident, except I believe this incident began my fear of spiders.

When I was five, we moved to another city, where we lived until I was nineteen. I had my own room by the time I was seven. My father woke me routinely at 7 a.m. by turning on my light and never saying a word. It was automatically my responsibility to wake my brothers for school, cook breakfast, make lunches, iron clothes (we didn't have permanent press then), and get us all to the school bus on time. I was in the first grade. My mother stayed in bed during this time because she felt that we fought too much. As I grew older, my responsibilities increased.

There was no loving affection in our home, no hugging or holding, but there were a lot of beatings. My mother beat me routinely, using a belt, shoe, stick, or anything other than her hands.

I don't know how old I was when my next molestation happened. Whenever I visited my cousin, my uncle came into her bedroom and slept with us. He began very gently to fondle me. The fondling increased gradually over the years into full intercourse and oral sex, and the "love affair" continued until I was twelve years old. During this time, I enjoyed considerable tenderness and affection from my uncle. He gave me the strokes that I was not receiving at home. I do think that the price was very high—my virginity—but it was worth it to me.

I looked forward to visiting my cousin because my relationship with my uncle meant kindness, affection, and yes, love-making. I don't remember what he said to prevent my talking. Maybe I was just afraid that someone would take him away from me. I felt very special, as if nobody in the world had what I had.

We were not permitted to discuss sex in our home. I had no idea that what was going on was wrong. I thought it was a special privilege. One day in school, I saw a movie about menstruation and birth. I was suddenly devastated when I discovered that I could get pregnant if, in fact, I was not already pregnant. I didn't know what to do or say. I let it slide and retreated further into myself.

A little later that year, we went to a barbecue at my uncle's house. I was reserved with him. Then my mother sent me out to find my brother, and I encountered my uncle alone in the back yard. I saw him and decided not to run from him. I told him that what he was doing to me was wrong and that I didn't want him to do that anymore. He said he wouldn't, and he never touched me again. Since I've been in therapy, I've realized that I had reached the age of noninterest to him. I believe that he preferred young children.

During this period of my life, I was also molested by a farm worker. I was nine years old and visiting at my grandfather's ranch. I remember lying on the floor in the bathroom, looking up at the scenes on the tub enclosure. I looked over my right shoulder and saw this man putting on his shirt as he was leaving the bathroom. I have blocked out the details, but I know what I was on the floor for.

My first love affair of my own choosing happened when I was four-teen, although I was forbidden to date until I was sixteen. The first time

Don and I made love, I was babysitting, and we were in the bedroom when the parents came home. Luckily for me, I always thought ahead. I had latched the chain on the door and they couldn't get in. Don and I dressed in a hurry, and I ran into the bathroom and flushed the toilet. As I went to the front door, Don went out the back door. We were safe. I told the baby's parents that they had caught me in the restroom, and they believed me.

When I was young, I was usually true to one guy at a time. That was my protection from being labeled a whore, as my mother would have called me. Whatever I wanted to do, I had to ask my mother. Most of the time, she refused. "The boys do," I always said. "They are boys," she replied. Then I asked to do something that boys didn't do, and she said, "Only whores do that!"

I was very confused about what I could and couldn't do. I wasn't a boy, and I didn't want to be labeled a whore. So I did the only things that I could get away with. I babysat kids from the time I was about eight until I graduated from high school. Since my mother allowed me to leave the house only when I was babysitting, I carried on secret love affairs at the same time. I always went with older guys because the boys my own age were ignorant about sex, and I just didn't like them young.

My big fantasy was to get married and live happily ever after. I had a false sense about life and marriage. When I met my first husband at the age of eighteen, it was love at first sight. Little did I know that he was already married, and when I did find out, somehow it didn't really matter. I made up my mind that I was going to marry him, and I did! We were married a year later, after his divorce, and just before he went to Vietnam. He was there during the entire thirteen months of our marriage. Eventually, things began to fall apart at home, conflicts with my in-laws, his taking their side, and other things. When I decided to end the marriage, he was in a war zone. I didn't want to tell him then. I met another man and started having an affair with him. When my husband came home from Vietnam, I told him about the affair; that ended the marriage. Sometimes I think I made a big mistake; I loved my first husband for twelve more long years after I divorced him.

The man who had been my lover became my second husband. At one point, I changed my mind about marrying him, but he talked me into going through with it. I felt trapped and resented him after that. I started belittling him in front of his friends. Eventually, I began to see the very behavior in myself that I so desperately hated in my mother. We had a baby because I had another fantasy, that a baby would improve our marriage. We got along all right, but we divorced when my son was two.

Anyone would think that, by this time, I had learned something, but I hadn't. That just shows how crazy and mixed up we AMACs can be. I had to add insult to my own injury. I had just met my best friend's brother-in-law, and we had a party. I was still living with husband number two; he came home and joined the party, we argued, and then we split up. In a little over a week, the man I had just met was living with me. I jumped from the frying pan into the fire. A year later, after I had divorced my second husband, I married number three. We had a fantastic relationship for six years, but then things got crazy. I was actually shocked about my decision to divorce him. I had really loved this guy. By that time, we had a daughter. She filled the void I still felt from the loss of my first marriage.

For the first time in my life, I was single, and I started a procession of relationships with guys. I got involved with an alcoholic/druggie and married him in Tijuana, thinking that the piece of paper was sort of a magic recipe. I still hadn't learned enough, but repeated my history. I found another alcoholic, and this time, the guy was crazy besides. He wanted me to go out and sell myself. I had a bad time with that suggestion because of the constant reminder from my mother: "Only whores would do that." I could give myself away, but I couldn't ask for money, or anything else. I did finally go out and find someone to proposition. I didn't ask for money. I only asked to get laid. In fact, I asked three different guys, who were all eagerly willing.

When I finally escaped that relationship, things got worse. All I could seem to pick were alcoholics or drug addicts, or both. I have no idea how many men I have been with in my life. Sex was just a tool. If a man wanted to take me out, he had to have sex with me. If he didn't want to have sex with me, I thought there was something wrong with me. It never occurred to me that it might be healthy to refrain from sex. I had been having sex with most of the men in my life for as long as I can remember. I was fortunate to have been spared diseases, and I never got pregnant until I was twenty. That pregnancy was aborted in Mexico. I had affairs with single men and with married men. It made no difference to me.

At last, I fell in love with another man. We met on my daughter's birthday, and six days later, when I saw him again, he asked me for my phone number. Since my phone was not hooked up, I told him I would go him one better. I gave him my address. He came over that night and moved in the next day. We married one year later. At this point, I had been divorced four years.

When we started living together, I decided to see a psychiatrist. I wanted to solve some of my problems with men. I had been through four divorces, and I didn't want another one. After three months, I stopped seeing this doctor because I didn't like her. After I married number five, things seemed to change in him. We have had a lot of rocky times. He is often withdrawn and doesn't share with me when things bother him. Instead, he goes to the bars and drinks, or just sulks. I wanted his affection and understanding. I began thinking something was wrong with me. We split up two or three times, and I had a brief affair with a man I had met in a bowling alley. He was kind and affectionate to me, and I craved that. It made me feel important, as if I were a real person again.

At one point, I was going to divorce number five and run off to Florida with my new lover. Then he led me into a program for spouses of alcoholics. There I met someone who introduced me to a group of people who had been sexually molested in childhood. After six months of treatment in that group, some of us have ventured off to form our new society, our new family, Adults Anonymous Molested As Children. I really identify with other AMACs. I can talk to them about anything. At this time in my life, I finally realize I have to face my problems and work through them. I chose to stay in my marriage and ended my affair.

Since I began therapy and joined AAMAC, my views about life and myself have changed drastically. I relate to other AMACs when they talk about how they are rebelling against the system. I am not alone in my feelings about taking care of other people without having others to take care of me. I am tired of having the responsibility of the house, laundry, meals, bills, and other burdens that go along with adulthood. I started being an adult when I was four years old and was never allowed to be a child. I don't understand children. My husband gets upset with me because I let my daughter do almost anything she wants. I don't make her do dishes, clean her room, or anything else that I had to do as a child. It is even hard for me to let her cook when she wants to. I want to do it all for her so she can enjoy her childhood. Her day will come too soon.

As for my son, now fifteen, he has lived with his father since he was eight years old. I was very loving to him until he was four. The older he got, the more like his father he looked. I hated his father, so I took it out on him. It is not my son's fault, and I try desperately to be nice to him when he comes to visit, but I can usually last only a few days. I love my son, but I have great difficulty dealing with him. I hated my brothers when we were young because they were boys. It is very hard for me to differentiate between my son and my brothers. I hope that one day he will understand that his mother does love him, but she has difficulty showing it.

I am just one of many AMACs in this giant world. Maybe in time, we can all completely recover.

13

YEP, I'M AN AMAC

I was born in wedlock to a middle-class family. By all social standards, I was a legitimate and bona fide blue-eyed bundle of joy. I nevertheless felt afraid when I was growing up, and angry at all of nature. I was not molested within my own family, but was mostly neglected by my parents and badmouthed by my older brothers. I was too young to hang around with them, and my parents were too busy to hang around with me. They worked hard, just trying to stay even. Nobody sang gentle lullabies to me. I often wondered why my parents waited five years to have their fourth child; perhaps I was an accident. I am here anyway, and out of sync with any game plans that may have been formed in my behalf.

Because nobody paid much attention to me, I had a lot of unsupervised time to explore life, and I did just that. My membership in AAMAC allows me now to examine my past and get used to the glimpses that reflection reveals. AAMAC also pulls me out of my addictive self-centered introspection, enabling me to serve other people in a healthy way. This service is truly a spiritual experience.

I am an adult who was molested as a child. Much of my life has been tragic, unique, and excessive. I truly am a fortunate survivor. The first sexual experiences I remember happened when I was eight or nine years old. My intuition hints about something at an even earlier age, but it has not surfaced yet.

I was first molested by pornographic literature. Whatever its intended audience, when children are exposed to pornography, that experience is a form of molestation. Damage to young minds can occur. Pornography molded my early sexual behavior and attitudes, which in turn influenced my disastrous adult life.

Twin sisters my own age and their brother two years older lived down the street from me. Their parents were out working their butts off, just like mine. The girls and their brother showed me some books they had found hidden in a cupboard above the refrigerator. They were hardcore erotic magazines and pornographic comic books known as "eight-page bibles." What a discovery! These books showed us everything we assumed we were supposed to do when we grew up. We didn't wait to grow up before we tried what the books showed us.

The four of us spent many hours imitating the sexual positions and acts the magazines depicted—all of them. Our sexual play soon became very sophisticated, and whatever we played had some kind of sexual connotation. When I was twelve years old, the other three children moved. Although I really hated to see them go, I had no idea what their absence would do to me. We had spent a great deal of time together for three years. Due to our sexual involvement, I didn't play very often with other children. Needless to say, my social skills were retarded, and my interests were quite advanced for kids my age. I was used to frequent sex, and I craved it. I was also by then, at the age of twelve, an alcoholic.

I entered puberty a short time after the twins moved. I was in the basement reading a hardcore pornographic booklet which, according to the introduction, was banned in the United States. What a joke! Nothing that makes money cannot be found in America. The book was quite explicit in both language and illustrations. As I was reading the torrid sex scenes, I suddenly felt a burning but ecstatic sensation in my genitals with a slight aching in my testicles. I barely got my penis out of my pants in time for the ejaculation. It smelled like sex and tasted a little salty. I really don't know why I tasted it, but I don't know why I tasted a girl's tears once either. Anyway, that was my big moment, in the basement, reading dirty books. I was too young to understand the true dynamics of sexuality and knew more than I should about sexual mechanics. But I was sure that sex felt good.

With the elation of climax to go along with everything else, I was really hooked now. All that I had seen and read in those books was now part of my personal sexual identity. I am amazed that society cannot admit that graphic sexual material does ruin a young person's mind. Kids today don't stand a chance of growing up unmolested in one way or another. Our society is sexually addicted and doesn't protect children from harm.

At the age of twelve, I had made my sexual obsessions and masturbation a way of life. My alcoholism was also becoming quite serious. I masturbated three or four times a day and drank whenever I could get alcohol. I was swirling in sexual fantasies and drunkenness. Some of the older kids in the neighborhood were gay. They often relieved my sexual frustrations and rewarded me with alcohol. I felt dirty and guilty for letting those guys go down on me, but the remorse didn't deter me.

That is the nature of obsessions: we sacrifice our self-worth for relief and fantasies that we cannot find in real life. While the boys were using me, I just conjured up a sexual fantasy with a girl, as though I were masturbating, which didn't feel as good, by the way. I even tried going down on a guy once when I was about fourteen. I was curious as to what they got out of doing it to me. I didn't care for it myself, but this experience made me feel even more guilty. It destroyed any masculine identity that might have been forming in me. These feelings didn't just go away either, but magnified as I grew up. At thirteen, I was already suffering from post-homosexual panic. The alcohol helped me to bury those feelings, or so I thought.

My formative years were obviously not the greatest. At the age of thirteen, I was raging in a blaze of alcoholism. I was a blatant pain in everybody's ass, as proud of my bad deeds as any high achiever was of good ones. I felt inadequate around girls because my desires and theirs didn't match. I knew it, and I felt guilty while knowingly fearing rejection. Girls that age didn't want a full-scale orgy twenty-four hours a day. They liked healthy things like going to football games and dancing, along with a couple of kisses and maybe a quick feel. Females were nonpersons to me. I saw them only as sexual objects. I was not growing up. I was eroding into adulthood, running away from myself and the law. Was I happy as a child? Was I happy as a teenager? Was I ever happy? I doubt it. My fondest memories of my childhood are X-rated and fogged with hangover after hangover. My feelings became so muddled that I couldn't separate them enough to define anything with clarity. I cared so much that, without proper upbringing, I had no choice but not to care at all.

Being molested as a teenager was much easier with the use and support of alcohol. The first perpetrator was a guy who sponsored me through a helping organization. Simply put, this guy bought me beer and gave me head. The beer helped ease the disgust I felt for myself, and the head relieved my sexual frustration for a while. It felt good, so what the hell. By the time I was seventeen, I had been molested many times: in bathrooms of movie theaters and other public places as a small child younger than twelve; in hobo jungles, where I used to hang out; by both men and women while hitchhiking. I had been arrested forty-two times by the age of seventeen, according to a police officer, and I had been molested many more times than that.

At seventeen, I was in jail again, awaiting transport to a boys' reformatory, when I had a spiritual experience. I made a sincere effort to turn to God for help with my troubled life. My friend suggested that I talk to a priest who was going to visit him that day. I accepted and was ready to commit myself to Catholicism. When we were alone with this guy, this so-called priest, he put his hands down the front of our pants and pulled us up to his crotch! All I can remember after that is my anger. I also felt deeply hurt and betrayed by God. I just went numb emotionally.

During my year's stay in the reformatory, my father died, and I had few visits from my family. I guess they shut me out. They never even knew the pain that I went through during my childhood and youth. How could I tell them? How could they ever understand?

So much for my tender formative years. From this point on, nothing that happened should surprise anyone. The little blue-eyed bundle of joy became a blue-eyed handful of pain, anger, mistrust, resentment, and bad attitudes, a powder keg of reactions and feelings born of trouble. At eighteen, I didn't know how to care or feel anything for other human beings. I was more or less emotionally dead inside and very much a loner. I had a transient nature and was incapable of close, feeling relationships with anything alive.

I deeply feared anyone's finding out about the things I had done in the past. I felt that I was a very bad person, different, not a complete man. I felt alienated and isolated and knew that nobody either cared or would understand. I sure as hell didn't understand. That reform school had done nothing to rehabilitate me. My trashy adult life reflected my early experiences. I became a male whore hustling the toughest streets in the world. I was also a drug addict and chronic alcoholic, the worst of both. To summarize years of misery, I did nine months in a mental institution, served honorably on a chain gang, spent forty-five days in solitary confinement on bread and water, lived for seven years on skid rows in many parts of America, beginning at the age of nineteen, and passed through many hospitals, missions, and detoxification centers across the country. I have been imprisoned in jails throughout the United States, Europe, and

Mexico, along with a couple of army stockades. I estimate my arrests to have numbered 250 or 300.

I have been off drugs and alcohol since December 1, 1975, and have spent several years in psychotherapy. I now hold several college degrees and a rich professional background in counseling and other human services. I have worked very hard to recover from my trauma-ridden past. But for years I interpreted that trauma only as childhood sexual experience, not as molestation. I blamed myself. It had been my own fault, I thought; I was responsible for what happened to me as an innocent child. I got what I wanted and my perpetrators got what they wanted. I didn't even know what an AMAC was. Despite my education and many internships in child protective services and social work, I never thought of myself as an AMAC!

I still had many interpersonal problems. I was still obsessed with sex. I continued in my anger-rage-hate cycles. I didn't trust organized religion or society at large. The list of destructive emotions goes on into infinity. I couldn't understand why, after all these years of psychotherapy, experience, education, and sobriety in a Twelve Step program, I still suffered these feelings and fears. Certainly, I thought, they should be gone by now.

I accepted a position as a co-therapist in a group of adults who were molested as children (not AAMAC). As my partner therapist interviewed me over the phone, I gave her some information about my personal background. She suddenly interrupted me and exclaimed, "Don't you realize that you are an AMAC? You were molested as a child!" I don't remember how I answered her, but her statement was burned into my brain. It was during my second week as co-therapist when the lights went on for me. I realized then that I too was an AMAC. I was molested so many times as a child that I cannot even count the acts, let alone remember all of them.

Since then, all of my painful feelings have ebbed considerably. I am healthier now than I have ever been before. I have come a long way in a very short time, thanks to many people, and thanks to AAMAC. I now accept the events of my life. I accept who I am today. I am damned proud of myself. I no longer live in subconscious denial. I no longer walk in the shadow of my perpetrators.

Elements of my old self will be with me for the rest of my life, to some degree, for I am the result of all that I have been to this very moment.

I understand now, however, what happened in my childhood. Now that understanding accompanies my feelings, I know where many of these feelings originated. I can do a lot to change them. AAMAC has taken me to new levels of awareness. There is still more for me to become. I have grown to love life and helping people to help themselves.

Adults Anonymous Molested As Children does work for those who want it.

14

I WAS ONLY FONDLED

Sexual matters were familiar to me at an early age. I had seen my parents have sex. I knew how to masturbate and get that tingly feeling. My dolls were also sexually active. And when I was six years old, my father was openly sexual with me.

My mother had gone grocery shopping, leaving my father and me alone together. He was sitting in a chair drinking and masturbating. I tried not to notice. He asked me to pull down my pants and come sit on his lap. I felt, "This is my daddy. He needs and expects this of me." He did not put his penis inside of me. He only fondled me and rubbed his penis near my vagina. I had not seen a penis that close before. I searched his face to see whether I was doing what he wanted me to do. Should I move or be still, I wondered.

Finally, he let me know that he was finished and I asked him whether I needed Mama's douche bag thing. He said no and told me not to tell Mother what had happened. I told on him anyway. I was afraid that he might try it again, and I felt that what he was doing was wrong.

At times my mother talked about leaving my father, but her religious values and financial dependency kept her from doing so. My mother and I were very close. She was always there to be my friend. She also recognized my musical talent and shielded me from my father. There was no affection other than sex expressed between my father and me—no pats, no hugs, no kisses or hand holding. He was harshly critical, cruel, and sarcastic sometimes, and spanked me severely when he was angry. Otherwise, he ignored me and was gone most of the time. I felt guilty for loving my mother and excluding my father from what she and I had together. I really thought that my father hated me, and I felt sorry that I had been born.

My father touched me other times, but only on the breasts. To be truthful, it felt good. His fondling of my breasts gave me a warm and contented feeling. He stopped touching me altogether after I was eight years old, but I continued masturbating. My mother shamed me when she caught me doing it. My father just let it go. I was always horrified when my mother caught me. When I asked her about sex, she said it hurt and was not fun for a woman. I got the message from her that it was somehow dirty or cheap for a woman to enjoy sex.

As I matured, life at home grew progressively worse, as if a disease had spread through the family. The symptoms were alcoholism, in both parents by then, fear, depression, violent outbursts, uneasy silence, hopelessness, isolation from other people, and some bestiality committed by my father on our pets.

It was a sorry background for my childhood and adolescence. I wanted to be like other kids, but I knew that my home life was vastly different from theirs. My mother used to catch me looking through my older brother's "girlie" magazines. I am uncomfortable admitting to what I am about to say, but I noticed that I had a particular attraction to the girls in these magazines. I have kept that secret for a very long time. I have always thought that such things were immoral and disgusting. The people I had seen naked at home were mainly women, however, and it is not at all shocking to me that I picked up my father's personal sexual obsession. I had seen a good deal of his hardcore pornography collection, which he may have thought was well hidden. I recall that some of his brown-paper-wrapped specials included pictures of children. As an adult, I now recognize that I have a choice, and I do not belittle myself for my sexual attraction to women. I have chosen not to act on those feelings, however, and I have decided that I prefer the company of men.

As I mentioned earlier, my father practiced bestiality. After he stopped touching me, his sexual interests shifted to animals, our pets. My dog died rather mysteriously. My mother suggested that maybe the big dogs got to her. I knew the truth, but never said anything. I had a special burial for her and I cried.

Another added attraction in my home life was the rough fighting between my mother and father. Once they were both naked and drunk. My father was demanding sex from my mom. He hit her, chased her, and then knocked her down the staircase once he had caught her. I can still hear my mother's cries and her head hitting each step. The abusive language was just as bad. I would cry and beg God to make it stop!

I was an overweight, acutely self-conscious teenager, teased a lot by the other kids. I had few friends and I felt insecure, ugly, and unwanted.

Today I may see a very pretty woman when I look in the mirror, but I still have serious doubts about my appearance and worth. As a teenager, I still masturbated, and I was very confused. I knew that what I did to myself felt good, but I felt cheap and dirty. My sense of what was right or acceptable contradicted what I had been taught. I slept with a large teddy bear until I was seventeen years old, and I held it very close. I lived in absolute fear of the next fight between my parents. Eventually my mother quit drinking and the fights diminished. My father was also gone a lot, and that certainly contributed to the new peace in the family.

I have had many ongoing problems in relationships with men. I am thirty-two now, and, although I have been engaged several times, I have never married. I always get involved with men who are unavailable or unsuitable in some way. Often, they are men who need my help; somewhere along the way, I go from being the rescuer to becoming the new victim. I believe that two people communicate the clues about their personalities before they speak a word to one another.

In one relationship, I was so deeply involved with a young man that our wedding plans were made. I had a wedding dress, and we had chosen a place for the ceremony. I was lost in a beautiful romantic dream. He backed out of the whole thing very suddenly and eventually determined that he was homosexual.

Then I met a man who was ten years older, a sober alcoholic. In many ways, the pain I experienced in this relationship surpassed that of my trauma-ridden childhood. I felt that I could somehow pull out of this relationship whenever I wanted to. He directed most of his rage at himself at first. He hit himself in the head or twisted his penis and said, "See what you do to me?" It didn't occur to me that he might eventually strike out directly at me. I would never end up like my mother, I thought, with an abusive man.

I was, of course, mistaken. He verbally abused me, beat me, and destroyed many of my personal things. I supported him, begged him publicly to come back to me, and ran after him down a busy highway at night. I used every enticement I could think of to keep him near me. I even offered to kill myself. He seemed interested in that prospect. I developed an obsession and became addicted to his leaving and my bringing him back. I also became addicted to his violence, our insanity, and the pain of that relationship. He also had other women during our two years together.

I am still trying to understand why I felt that I deserved such degradation. Not only did I feel that I deserved it, but I enjoyed it! I suspect that this man represented my father and my desperate struggles to win his love and approval. When that relationship ended, I surrendered. I suffered from deep depression and a sense of loss. I realized that I had denied reality for too long.

Now I am eager for a clear perception of the truth. I must change, and my recovery is a high priority with me. I read to learn all that I can. I have begun psychotherapy and joined a program for friends and relatives of alcoholics. I am trying to reprogram myself with positive messages and am vigilant against the negative statements I silently make about myself that can destroy any good I might feel about my character and accomplishments. My self-doubt is strong, but no stronger than the belief in myself that I am developing. I have not rushed into another relationship to fix me. I also joined AAMAC. It is good for me to know that other people have had experiences similar to mine.

We in AAMAC are all at different levels of recovery. We are all here to listen and share without judgment, but with compassion. It is a revelation honestly to exchange ideas and feelings, particularly with those AMACs who are perpetrators. The insights and different perspectives they provide are invaluable because greater understanding brings greater peace of mind, fewer resentments, less anger, and less pain. This relief is refreshing after all my years of suffering.

When I first began attending AAMAC, I felt very intimidated. Little by little, I have revealed and accepted the truth about myself. I have grown close to people in my workshop. Despite all that they know about me, they still accept me and love me just as I am. AAMAC is helping me discover beauty and talents and capabilities. We have a strong bond of trust among ourselves, and I recognize these people as real friends. The growth that I have achieved has had its price. It is slow and painful. I still resist opening some of those closed doors of my childhood. But I know that the only way out of pain is through it. When I confront my fear, it loses its power to dominate my life. That is the heart of the matter in Adults Anonymous Molested As Children.

15

THE TRUTH ABOUT ME

I spent most of my boyhood and youth being afraid, confused, and angry. I thought that it was normal to feel that way. I observed that adults were not happy either, especially married adults. It seemed to me that people were happy only when they were having sex. Love was just a four-letter word that everybody spoke a lot but never understood. To me, love and sex were the same. You couldn't have one without the other, but, to be respectable, you must first be married.

I discovered later that love and sex were not the same. I learned that sex was wrong and love was good. If you were married, then sex was allowed. I thought that women would only use me for their own selfish needs and desires. I felt worthless and unredeemable because I had had oral sex with another man and because I thought about sex a lot; to me, thinking was the same as doing.

During the first sexual experience I remember, I was trying to do to my brother what the man and woman were doing in the bed next to ours. I was very young and had been told falsely that these people were my parents. When I got on top of my brother and started moving as the man in the bed did, my brother woke up and began to cry. My "parents" chastised me severely and told me that I was doing something wrong. I was really traumatized by their disapproval of my early childhood curiosity. Shortly afterward, these people gave my brother and me away to a woman I later learned was my grandmother. We were taken to a new home, where we were introduced to our grandfather, aunt, and real mother. Other family members also moved in and out frequently.

I learned that my aunt had been adopted out of an orphanage. At this time, she was about eight years old, and her brother was allowed to visit her. While he was at our house visiting my aunt, he spent a good deal of his time teaching me how to suck him. He explained to me that this was our secret. I remember that he was about ten years old at that time. Eventually, my aunt, my brother, and I were left with another family in town. My grandparents and mother went away to work as harvesters. I don't remember much about my stay there except that I had a bed-wetting problem. My aunt and the daughter of the people we were staying with shamed me for it. They also liked to taunt me and tickle me. I was so ticklish that I would lose my breath and wet my pants every time they tickled me. Once when I had wet the bed, my grandmother put me in a diaper and sent me outside for everyone to see what a baby I was. When anyone asked why I was wearing a diaper, I had to answer, "Because I wet my bed."

My own and another family eventually moved back into the country. The others had a daughter about my age, and we used to play sex games. When somebody caught us, the girl's family moved away. It was also at this time when I was caught sleeping with a life-size doll between my legs. The adults punished me severely again, and I was forbidden to play with dolls alone after that incident. I was also caught climbing on top of my aunt while she was taking a nap. She awoke and called out for help. I was taken into the living room, where my mom smeared vaseline all over my penis while my entire family watched. At this time of my life, my mother spent a good deal of time curling my hair to "make me look pretty." She also pierced my ears and put dresses on me.

Adults at school also treated my normal sexual experiences in damaging ways. Once I was caught kissing a girl in the Boys' Waiting Lounge. The teacher placed me in front of the class where she could watch me. She also publicly chastised me and segregated me from the other boys. Another time, after school, a girl told me that, if I could catch her, I could kiss her. I couldn't catch her, but another boy did. He tripped her, which gave me enough time to catch up to her, kiss her, and run away. My aunt told my grandmother, who convinced me that the girl's father would hunt me down and horsewhip me. Eventually I became unwilling to play kissing games and the like because I felt that sex was a sin and a crime for which there was no forgiveness.

At the same time, I wondered why older kids and adults could enjoy sex, but I couldn't. My mother brought her boyfriends home and took them to bed. Even though they closed the curtain, I could hear what was going on, and I could watch them. During those years, my mother and grandmother were always fighting. They threw dishes in one of their fights. I witnessed other violence in my home too. I watched my mother almost kill a man. Another time, I watched a different man beat my mother into unconsciousness. These were men we lived with.

When we moved away from my grandmother to another town, we lived with a man who I understood was my father. Once he and I were lying naked on the bed in our one-room apartment when a woman friend of my mother came to visit. My mother told us to cover up, and the man refused. "Let her come in if she wants to," he said, "but we're not moving." The lady became obstinate and flustered before she left.

This man, my father, was eventually fired from his job for leaning on his shovel too much, and my mother then left him. We moved in with a different man in another town, and my brother came to stay with us again. My mother and her boyfriend often went out at night and left us with two girls. We showed our bodies to each other and touched a lot. My brother was also involved, but he didn't understand what was really going on.

At the age of ten, while I was living in yet another town with my grandmother, my aunt's brother came to visit. We spent our nights together, playing with each other and ourselves. The preacher's son taught us how to masturbate. I believe it was at this age when I was also raped at a public swimming pool by an adult male, who assaulted me anally. Other sexual encounters included my being forced to suck a group of boys to a point of climax. And I was beaten by six older boys who then urinated in my face. At the time of these terrible experiences, I was taking care of my grandfather, who suffered from Parkinson's disease. I was ordered to take him to the bathroom, hold his penis, and clean him off after he went.

The patterns and themes of my childhood are evident in these memories—frequent moves in and out of different families; bed-wetting; masturbating a lot and being caught and punished; and various other sexual experiences that were associated with violence, shame, or both. I became a loner and withdrew into myself.

By the age of twelve, I hated people, including my own family. I had been accused of committing crimes against girls, stealing, arson, malicious mischief, and murder. I couldn't trust anyone because everyone always wanted something from me and gave me nothing in return. I received clothes at Christmas. The rest of the time, most of everything was given to my brother. I remember my mother and grandmother telling one of their friends that I wasn't a lovable person. My grand-mother was always saying that I shouldn't try to go to college because I wasn't bright enough. I was made to work from the age of nine.

I hated people, for sure. I wanted a new world. I didn't want to marry, but I did want a baby girl in order to raise my own companion. She would have been trained to be a lady and never to hurt anyone's feelings. She would be affectionate. I wanted girls to like me, and I wanted to like them. They liked other boys, kissed them, petted with them, and even had sex with them, but not with me. I knew it was wrong, and I was afraid of them. Then, when I was fifteen, I met a girl who liked me. We were both interested in religion and medicine. We even kissed on occasion. I told her that I loved her. My grades went from Ds and Cs to Bs and As. We planned to complete our education and become medical missionaries in service to God.

When I joined the army to learn a trade, while I was in basic training, my girlfriend married our minister's son. I shipped out to Germany, met a German girl, and stayed married to her for twelve years. When I found out that she was having affairs, I asked her to stop. She refused and told me to leave. I felt betrayed again, and I was very hurt over the whole thing.

Then I met my second wife. She was beautiful and intelligent (though a little scatterbrained), but it seemed to me that all she wanted me for was to work and bring home the money. Things got bad, and money was short. Life at home was becoming really difficult for us. I am not sure how or why it happened, but I started fondling my daughter. My wife was spending a lot of time away from home, so it was easy enough to do. I continued fondling her for about six months. When she asked me to stop, I did, but she later reported me to the authorities. I confessed, was convicted of a felony, and sent to jail.

In all of my struggles to be accepted, I have failed. I have done the unforgivable. I have molested my daughter. My punishment, besides jail, will be to go on living and trying to get better. I have learned that there is no cure for people like me, but we can recover. I am destined to be forever scorned by my society, and I'm afraid that I will go to hell, but while I'm alive I must keep trying to improve myself.

16

DAD MADE ME WATCH

My memories begin when I was about five years old and small for my age. My parents always called me stupid because I wasn't good at school. My friends and I envied the gang leaders who were bigger and had more guts than we did.

When I was about seven, we lived in a two-story house, where I used to watch my parents from the stairs. They drank every night and played around on the couch. I got my sister one night and showed her what our parents were doing. After that, she and I played house a lot. I believe that this sex play was a result of seeing what our parents were doing. I also started losing respect for them at about this same time.

My parents argued a lot when I was about ten, and Mom started wearing see-through blouses. I was afraid to look, but at the same time, I felt excited. That double emotion stayed with me, right up to the present. I felt guilty about my feelings, and I believe that is why I'm shy around women.

I learned to disrespect my dad for the way he treated my mother. I believe that's where my rebellious nature comes from. My mother always gave in to my dad in the arguments. I was also lonely and couldn't talk to my friends about what was going on at my house. I tried to talk to my grandparents, but I beat around the bush and couldn't get the words to come out. My parents always told me to keep the sex in the family. Since I couldn't talk about it to anyone, I just kept it to myself and lived with it. That's the way I was as I grew up. I was really a mixed-up kid.

I was twelve or thirteen when my family started camping a lot in the desert, out in the middle of nowhere. We rode motorcycles during the day and played cards at night. My mom ran around topless with loose bottoms or with her blouse opened all the way. My dad was always caressing her in a sexual way. This behavior made me uncomfortable, but the worst thing for me was my dad's questioning what I thought about my mom's breasts. I realize now that I both liked and disliked seeing them.

Dad put words in my mouth until I nodded in agreement with whatever he was saying, or until he got tired of asking me the questions.

Once when our family was out in the desert, Dad and I went for a bike ride. Before the ride, I felt relaxed and happy. Then we pulled over to the side of the road, and I could tell that we were going to have another "father-and-son talk." He asked me what I thought about Mom's breasts. I couldn't answer him. He asked whether I liked them, and I must have nodded. I remember the fear of being confronted by him. That's something I never want to go through again.

He kept badgering me until I finally agreed that I thought Mom had pretty breasts. Then we went back to the tent and played cards. Dad asked me again, in front of Mom, whether I thought she had pretty breasts. I nodded. He wanted to hear me say it; in whispers and with great fear, I did. After that, he got off my back and I felt better for a little while. After dinner, we played more cards. Then my dad asked me to play with my mom's breasts. She didn't say anything, even though she didn't approve. I shook my head to refuse. He kept pushing me, but my mom stepped in and told him to stop it. I think she did that because she sensed my nervousness and fear. In all my twenty-seven years, I have never experienced such extreme fear as I felt that night. I survived that camping trip, but my disrespect for my dad worsened from that time on.

It seems that every day, when I returned home from school, Mom and I started yelling at one another. I never cried from the spankings she and Dad gave me. I just didn't care. Once my mom and I were yelling, and she chased me into the garage. I picked up a .22-caliber rifle barrel as if it were a baseball bat. I raised it at her, but I never swung it. She stopped, and I put the gun barrel down and calmly walked away. She never came after me again. She still says that she thinks I would have hit her. I don't know, but I think that maybe I loved her too much to do something like that, even though I didn't respect her.

We moved to a nicer town when I was about fifteen. By now I believed that you looked out for yourself. You carried knives or chains to school and belonged to a gang. I found myself in a school with nice buildings, well-dressed students, and no gangs, but I still didn't change my ideas. I started drinking, doing drugs, cutting school, and running away. I found a new love in drinking and drugs. I didn't respect anything, or care for anyone, including myself. I was kicked out of that school and went to a continuation school where everyone partied. I was a hardcore drinker by the time I was eighteen.

Then my family moved to the desert. That's when my dad made it okay for me to drink beer. I started running around with people who felt pretty much the same about themselves as I did. We were always drinking and raising hell around town. I had a lot of cars, but they didn't last long. I also suffered hopelessness and was a thief. My parents tried to talk to me, but whatever they said went in one ear and right out the other. When I got drunk, I told my father what I felt about him. We usually ended up in a fist fight, and I usually lost. Finally, I stole his motorcycle and wrecked it. I didn't feel any pain until the next day. I was kicked out of the house for that.

Before this last incident, my sister and I were still having our sex, and I was still seeing my mom's breasts. Mostly, my sister and I just had foreplay, but a couple of times when I was drunk, she gave in and we went all the way. Once I tried to force her and stopped because the phone rang. Next thing I knew, my sister came out of the bathroom wearing a towel and teasing. Then I didn't want any sex.

I had always masturbated a lot. In fact, I had done it just about every night since I first started watching my parents play their little sex games. I was always horny, and I still am. After I was kicked out of the house, I moved in with a friend, a thirty-two-year-old wino. My rent was a bottle of whiskey or wine a month. My favorite pastimes were feeling sorry for myself, drinking, and killing flies all day. I was fired from my job for stealing, and spent time in jail for my first drunk driving charge. I didn't like myself. I joined the Job Corps in Oregon and spent three months working forestry duty. During that time, I drank only one quart of beer. I remember that I didn't want to maintain my cool; I wanted more beer. After that, I joined the army in Portland, Oregon. I was on my way now—out on my own in the real world.

After I joined the army, I remember going to an adult book store and watching the dirty movies. I was in a private booth once masturbating when a man walked in. He didn't say much of anything. He started playing with me and then gave me head. It felt good and, at that time, I didn't feel any shame, but after I climaxed, I left that place fast. I didn't want to return the favor. I ran from the book store to the hotel room, looking back occasionally to make sure no one was following me.

During my first three years in the army, I was always in trouble. After basic training and military school training, I returned to my home state. I began visiting adult book stores about once a month. I had sex with a variety of men, but they had to give me alcohol before I would let them do anything to me. I never felt right about it and was always ashamed. But I was too shy to find a girl. I felt that women wouldn't want me anyway. I drank too much and got into a lot of trouble.

I did enough drinking and driving to log three drunk driving arrests by the age of twenty-two. My last was a blackout while I was on my way to the book store. The police report said that I had run a red light and driven over a center divider curb. I then ran a stop sign, crossed over two lanes of highway and hit a tree. That was when I gave up on myself. The car I was driving was only three months old, and already I had driven 20,000 miles and had three accidents.

The judge gave me six months in jail or the alternative of a live-in recovery program for alcoholism. This sentence was the beginning of a new way of life for me. I learned that I didn't have to drink after I accepted a little bit of truth about myself. I also discovered that I wasn't gay. I was just horny and lonely. I attended an anonymous alcohol treatment program and stayed sober one day at a time. My life improved, and I really learned a lot about myself. I felt good about myself for the first time ever. It's a strange feeling to a guy like me—not being afraid of everything and everyone because of the things that happened in my past.

After being sober for about three years, I found that I had more problems than just alcoholism. I still had a lot of fear, nervousness, and feelings of being inferior to everybody else. While sharing with a friend one night, I realized that I had a lot of hate toward my parents for the terrorizing fear they implanted in me when I was growing up. I knew that there was more than just hate in me. There was anger, mistrust, insecurity, and defiance. I see now that I am an AMAC. I am the only person responsible for how I handle my adult life. The shame I learned as a child belonged to the perpetrators. But I am responsible today for changing my attitudes.

Today, I like the word "reality" because I'm not the same person I was five years ago, lost in drugs, alcohol, and sex. Today, I seek the real truth about myself. I try to change my faults by understanding what I'm all about without blaming myself unnecessarily. Today, I'm not in dreamland, wishing for the world. I am proud of myself and I am achieving goals and doing things I never thought I could do, one day at a time. I found that I am not a bad person, and I'm not stupid. Most important, I am responsible for my actions.

This essay is the truth about me. I hope other people who read it, and who have walked in my shoes, are honest with themselves and willing to escape their misery as I have done. The truth does set me free, and the more real I become, the fewer head games I play. I can honestly say that I love you all. I pray that, if you relate to my story, you will join us in Adults Anonymous Molested As Children and enjoy a better way of life.

3

THE AAMAC
ORGANIZATION

17

WORKSHOP INFORMATION AND GUIDELINES

Registration of AAMAC Workshops

It is very important for several reasons that new workshops register with the national organization, AAMAC WSO, Inc. In order to estimate how much literature to print and to gauge when we're large enough to institute general service conferences and publish national directories, we must know how large our population is. Registration of workshops in our WSO allows us to mail announcements and otherwise to communicate with each other. We therefore urge you, after your workshop has existed for ninety days, to register without delay.

Proper Listing of AAMAC Workshops

In order to minimize confusion as we grow, we have devised some general procedures to help us maintain uniformity in our records. New workshops personalize themselves with names to distinguish one from another. The parent organization, however, goes by the workshop's Registration Number (RN), not by its name. When you register with AAMAC WSO, Inc., we will assign the Registration Number. It will help us immensely if you use this number in all communications.

Here are some examples of names and RNs:

VICTOR VALLEY GROUP: RN [0-0-000-0-G] 0-00-00-0-A
AAMAC Workshop: Bookstudy/Participation
0000 N. Blank St.
Your Town, State Zip
Meets: Friday (7 p.m. to 9 p.m.)
Secretary: Carolyn J.

EAST SIDE GROUP: RN [0-0-000-0-S] 0-00-00-0-A
AAMAC Workshop
0000 N. Blank Ave.
Your Town, State Zip
Meets: Tuesday (7 p.m. to 9 p.m.)
Secretary: Jack J.

NORTH SIDE GROUP: RN [0-0-000-0-S] 0-00-00-0-A
AAMAC Workshop: Rotating Workshop
0000 N. Blank Blvd.
Your Town, State Zip
Meets: Thursday (7 p.m. to 9 p.m.)
Secretary: John S.

WHAT THE WORKSHOP REGISTRATION NUMBER TELLS AAMAC

RN [5-5-001-1-S] 6-86-91-5-A

STATE ....[5
REGION...5
ORDER OF REGISTRATION 001
NUMBER OF WORKSHOPS................1
S = SINGLE WORKSHOP ....S]
G = GROUP ....
MONTH FIRST REGISTERED.............6
YEAR FIRST REGISTERED 86
CURRENT YEAR REGISTERING......91
YEARS IN EXISTENCE 5
A = ACTIVE..A
I = INACTIVE...

The first space of the sample RN (Registration Number) above, [5, tells us that there is an AAMAC workshop in California, the fifth state of the United States in alphabetical order.

RN [5-

The second space in the RN (Registration Number), -5-, tells us that this particular state is located in Region Five.

RN [5-5-

The third space in the RN (Registration Number) is a series of numbers, -001-, which records the numerical order in which the workshop registered with AAMAC WSO, Inc., relative to the registration of the first AAMAC workshop.

RN [5-5-001-

The fourth space in the RN (Registration Number), -1-, tells us the number of workshops under this workshop's specific name. Generally, a group has more than one workshop within its fold, meeting on various nights. However, they all identify as part of the same group. For instance, a workshop decides to have one type of AAMAC workshop on one night, and a different kind on another night. While they meet on different nights for different workshops, they all have a single RN (Registration Number).

RN [5-5-001-1-

The fifth space in this RN (Registration Number), -S], tells us that this is a single workshop. If two or more workshops used the same name, we would classify them as a group, -G].

RN [5-5-001-1-S]

The sixth space of the RN (Registration Number), here, -6-, tells us in which month the workshop first registered with AAMAC.

RN [5-5-001-1-S] 6-

The seventh space of the RN (Registration Number), -86-, tells us the year in which the workshop first registered with AAMAC.

RN [5-5-001-1-S] 6-86-

The eighth space in this example, -91-, tells us the last year in which the workshop registered. This shows whether the registration is current and whether the workshop is -A] (Active) or -I] (Inactive). Only currently registered workshops are considered active. Of course, we will send reminders to register when we see that a registration has lapsed. It is very important that a workshop maintain active registration in order to receive important announcements and other related information from AAMAC. Otherwise, the workshop will be removed from the mailing list.

RN [5-5-001-1-S] 6-86-91-

The ninth space in the RN (Registration Number), -5-, tells us at a glance how many years the workshop has been in existence.

RN [5-5-001-1-S] 6-86-91-5-

The tenth space in the RN (Registration Number), the letter -A, tells us at a glance the status of your workshop, whether active -A or inactive -I.

RN [5-5-001-1-S] 6-86-91-5-A

Now, when we run this registration number through our computer, it provides us with a great deal of information and takes up very little space otherwise. What does it all translate into besides efficiency and considerable financial savings?

RN [5-5-001-1-S] 6-86-91-5-A tells us that:

In the state of California, which is located in our Region Five, the first AAMAC workshop began in June 1986. This workshop is registering in 1991, which means that it is in its fifth year of existence, and, since 1991 is also the current year, is still active. When we cross coordinate the RN to our mailing list, it tells us that the name of this workshop is the "Original Founders' Group" and its address. Since the workshop is active, we will leave it on our current mailing list. Were it inactive, we would remove it from our current mailing list and our next directory. Of course, we would first try to contact the workshop, just in case the registration for the current year was overlooked.

As you can see, it is very important to keep your RN current in order to remain on our Active listing. Always include your RN with any correspondence you may have with AAMAC. We go by the RN and not by the workshop name because of the possibility of duplication. Your RN tells us that you exist and provides us with the privilege of serving you. You may initially register your workshop at any time; try thereafter to register every year in June, our census month, when we are especially geared for any changes that we need to make in AAMAC as a whole. Your cooperation will greatly help us all.

SECRETARY'S GUIDE

Effectively serving the needs of your workshop is very easy, but the Secretary should understand some general policies of the AAMAC World Services Office, Inc., the guardian of our traditional AAMAC program.

AAMAC is a writing, printing, publishing, and distribution society concerned with the recovery of AMACs and the carrying of our message to AMACs who still suffer. Our guidelines are the Twelve Steps, Twelve Traditions, and Five Legacies.

The general AAMAC Program will comprise three books. This book, ADULTS ANONYMOUS MOLESTED AS CHILDREN, is our main text, in which we explain in a general way who we are, what we are about, what happened to us in the past, and what we are like now. We recommend that every member of our AAMAC society own a copy of this text and, preferably, all our publications.

STEP BY STEP, to be published, will serve as our daily guide to progress. This book provides serious members with a path to follow. It offers AMACs food for thought and helps prime them to think for themselves. This book offers an approach to working the Twelve Steps, Twelve Traditions, and Five Legacies by putting them into action.

WORKSHOP INFORMATION AND SERVICE GUIDELINES, to be published, is our service manual and the workshop personal records book, combined in one volume. All pertinent information is in this book: AAMAC Charter, General Service Conference structure, meeting records, registration forms, and workshop formats. Always have some current copies on hand. Until this book is available, let this supplement be your guide for getting started.

As a society of AMACs, we advise all of our members to enter some type of private therapy in conjunction with their working the AAMAC program. Therapy greatly assists and speeds recovery.

All AAMAC workshop business should be discussed in the Steering Committee Meeting, rather than during the regular hours of the workshop, lest we be diverted from our primary purpose. Such a Steering Committee could meet before or after the regular workshop, or at another time in a member's home. A Steering Committee is a small group of elected members who attend a workshop regularly and consider it their home group. We hope that these trusted servants will show a capacity for a level head, know the WORKSHOP INFORMATION AND SERVICE GUIDELINES, and harbor no desire to become authority figures. These three to six elected servants include the Secretary, Treasurer, and one or two senior members of the workshop. They function by guidance of the group conscience through a raising of hands or by ballot. The rest of the Steering Committee Meeting includes all interested members who consider that workshop to be their home group and attend regularly. Each workshop is autonomous and manages its own affairs. Members do not go to another AAMAC workshop and vote on issues of that group. Furthermore, each member of AAMAC should have only one home group where she or he does all of her or his voting, about AAMAC as a whole or otherwise. The term of service for any trusted servant should be from six months to one year.

Brief announcements often conclude a meeting. These are not to be confused with group business. More serious matters should be handled in the Steering Committee Meeting. We do not attend regular AAMAC workshops to take care of meeting business. We are here to share our experience, strength, and hope, and to meet new people coming into the program. Nothing turns off a prospective member more quickly than to go to a workshop expecting to deal with AMAC problems and to find instead controversy and boring details about things he or she knows nothing about.

AAMAC workshops last two hours and meet once weekly, or, in the case of a group under the workshop's umbrella, two or more nights a week. We support ourselves through our own contributions. We use our monies for purchasing literature, buying supplies, and donating to the AAMAC WSO, Inc. society. At the end of each workshop, while the Secretary makes any brief announcements concerning AAMAC as a whole, we pass the collection basket. Then the Secretary asks for any announcements from the general membership. That being done, everyone stands and joins hands for a moment of silent meditation for AMACs who still suffer and for all those who suffer from child abuse.

Many of us like to get together after a workshop and compare experiences or just have some laughs and congenial conversation, exchange phone numbers, and so on. These casual gatherings help us strengthen friendships and allow us to pick up any loose ends left over from the workshop. We generally meet at a favorite restaurant or coffee shop.

We close our workshops to the general public, spouses of AMACs, children, relatives, and researchers. The nature and content of our discussions is reason enough to do so. We answer to nobody but ourselves. AMACs are uncomfortable and apprehensive about sharing in the presence of nonmembers. It is tough enough for many of us to share with other AMACs, let alone outsiders. The AAMAC workshop is set aside exclusively for AMACs and those who are deciding whether they are AMACs. We do not allow the attendance of any member of an outside agency, whether it be a court of law, social service agency, or probation office. We have no opinions on outside issues. We are exclusively for AMACs, lest we be diverted from our primary purpose. Our workshops do not affiliate themselves with any outside group or agency. We may participate in seminars or other public functions, so long as we do so in cooperation, without affiliation. We are not a secret society, and we do speak at the public level, but we never discuss other members outside of AAMAC or use their names.

Use of the AAMAC Workshop Preamble is crucial to the rights of our members and others. This protects anyone attending the workshop from disclosing information that might be used against him or her. We are a helping society of AMACs working with AMACs. The Preamble helps us to ensure that everyone in the group understands our commitment to obey the laws regarding child abuse and disclosure. Should you have further questions, be sure to write us. Always include a self-addressed, stamped envelope if you wish a reply. Many workshop discussion topics can be found in our literature. We are a working program, concerned about how our AMAC past has carried over into controlling our adult lives. We are smashing our secrets, and some ventilation about those who have wronged us is necessary, but we need not be obsessed with that issue alone.

Use of the AAMAC name is a granted privilege, not a right. AAMAC is a voting society in the same tradition as other anonymous programs. An AAMAC workshop has authority over itself, and votes by majority. Members also vote on issues regarding their General Service Conference structure. We do not change general AAMAC policy at the workshop level. We must at least stay within the guidelines of what constitutes an

AAMAC workshop. Although our Traditions are meant only as suggestions, we try to stay within their framework. Should a workshop deviate
from our tried and proven path, cease practicing our program of recovery, become immersed in problems other than AMAC issues, bring in
professional psychotherapists and practice psychotherapy as a workshop
function, start charging fees, sell other than AAMAC literature at its
workshops, or conduct itself in ways that reflect badly on the AAMAC
society as a whole, the General Service Conference or the AAMAC World
Services Office, Inc. may remove its privilege to use the AAMAC name.
We are not affiliated with any other anonymous program, and all workshops are autonomous except in matters affecting AAMAC as a whole.

We do encourage individual workshops to try new ideas and new
types of interactions. However, we also expect those workshops to keep
in mind that the eyes of the world are upon us and watching our progress.
Let us know what new approaches are working for your workshop. If you
have questions about staying within the AAMAC guidelines, write us.
You will find we are quite liberal and open-minded. We are eager to assist
you in any way we can, and want your suggestions for improving the program. Please keep in touch with us.

AAMAC is coming from poor and humble beginnings. We prefer
to see the price for our literature as a request for much-needed donations.
We depend on these donations and contributions from the workshops
to help us survive and to carry the message to AMACs who still suffer.
Never send cash. Make checks or money orders out to AAMAC WSO,
Inc. Our mailing address is:

AAMAC WSO, Inc.
P.O. Box 662
Apple Valley, CA 92307

Keep in mind that recovery from any problem stands on a foundation
of honesty and truth, which result in true integrity, the key to healing.

We have many informative publications forthcoming. All registered
workshops will be notified when these materials become available. In
order to register your AAMAC workshop, simply contact AAMAC WSO,
Inc. and let us know where and who you are. Be sure to include a business-size, self-addressed, stamped envelope. Once you receive your Reg-

istration Number, be sure to include it with all further correspondence to AAMAC.

To protect individual anonymity, all of our shipments and correspondence will be labeled with only the P.O. box number as our return address. We ask that you order materials in bulk as much as possible. Be sure to order a new WORKSHOP INFORMATION AND SERVICE GUIDELINES every June (census month) when you renew your workshop's registration. Any new information and forms will be there, along with the usual workshop records for the Secretary.

We will eventually print national directories of AAMAC workshops. Registering yours and updating any necessary information is critical to keeping these directories accurate. It would be terrible for an AMAC seeking help to show up for a workshop that is no longer active, or that has moved.

This is the general background that any trusted servant of AAMAC should know. For that matter, any member of AAMAC would be wise to learn all about the society in order to protect it and serve effectively. The General Service Conference structure, once it is activated, is the deciding body and the collective voice of the AAMAC workshops. Learn to love it and know its functions, for it is your guarantee to participation in AAMAC as a whole. To do less would be to withhold your part in the program. That would truly be a misunderstanding and personal victimization of yourself.

DUTIES OF TRUSTED SERVANTS AT THE WORKSHOP LEVEL

Secretary

The general caretaker of the workshop arrives early enough to set up meeting place and make coffee. Chooses Leader for the evening. Secures meeting place after meeting. Keeps workshop records up to date and serves on the Steering Committee. Also schedules special meetings as necessary to take care of group business. Term of service is six months or preferably one year.

Treasurer

The Treasurer counts money after collection is passed and enters amounts into group records. Makes deposits into established workshop checking account. Makes financial report to workshop monthly. Handles donation of monies to AAMAC General Service Conference, and local Central Office as directed by group conscience. Obtains two of three authorized signatures for all checks. Serves on Steering Committee. Term of service is six months or preferably one year.

Literature Representative

Keeps larger workshops supplied with adequate amount of literature. Term of service is unlimited. Does not serve on Steering Committee.

Steering Committee

Three to six elected trusted servants, including Secretary, Treasurer, and one or two senior members, and all other interested members who consider the workshop to be their home group and who attend regularly. Meets as needed, but at least once quarterly, to oversee coming problems or business that may need attention. Considers all detailed business and problems of any magnitude. Never, under any circumstances, keeps secrets from the general workshop membership; everything that relates to the group is their business. Trusted servants serve the group; never do they govern.

TYPES OF AAMAC WORKSHOPS

PREAMBLES, PROCEDURES, AND FORMATS

- Question-and-Answer Workshop
  (Closed to the Public)
- Bookstudy/Participation Workshop
  (Closed to the Public)
- Twelve Step Workshop
  (Closed to the Public)
- Rotating Workshop

The workshop may elect to use a combination of meetings or stay with a single type of weekly meeting. Whatever you decide, we have a standardized format to guide you as you establish your workshop. Feel free to improvise it to your own liking. However, we ask you not to deviate from certain guidelines. For historical purposes, the name "Original Founders' Group" has been reserved for the first AAMAC workshop. We ask that no other AAMAC workshop use this one name. There can be only one, and it is located in Victorville, California. It is the parent to all other workshops, since all that we are began there.

Groups other than AAMAC who include a number of AMAC members may wish to organize AAMAC workshops, but not be diverted from their original purpose. Such special-interest groups are welcome. You need not jeopardize your own primary focus by holding an AAMAC workshop under your umbrella. We ask only that your AAMAC workshop function with integrity regarding AAMAC as a whole and return the support we give you. If we can serve you, please write us and let us know. Always include a business-size, self-addressed, stamped envelope for a response. We are certain that AMACs need treatment for their condition as AMACs, regardless of other needs or group involvement. Experience in AAMAC usually complements treatment for related problems, disorders, or symptoms. Here are examples of special-interest AAMAC groups:

AAMAC Workshop: First Baptist Church Group
AAMAC Workshop: Gay and Lesbian Group
AAMAC Workshop: Addicts in Recovery Group

AAMAC WSO, Inc. tries to assist related groups in a spirit of cooperation, without affiliation. We only want to reach AMACs who still suffer, and are willing to go to any lengths to do so. We have no interest in trying to cure all ills. Consider our primary purpose and help us to reach out. Please allow six to eight weeks for a response to your inquiry. We are just beginning to reach out nationally, are understaffed, and operating on a limited budget. Thank you.

AAMAC STANDARD WORKSHOP FORMAT

1. LEADER BEGINS MEETING: My name is _____ and I am an adult who was molested as a child. Welcome to our AAMAC workshop. Please help yourself to the refreshments and pamphlets. If you wish to purchase any literature, please see the Literature Representative or Secretary. Let's introduce ourselves. Please state only your first name and the nature of your problem (My name is _____ and I am an AMAC).

   Is there anyone here for the first, second, or third AAMAC workshop? Please introduce yourself by first name only and state the nature of your problem. We offer you a special welcome. New members are the lifeblood of our program. We want you to know that you never have to be alone again. We care about you and will do all that we can to help you.

2. SECRETARY PASSES AROUND PHONE NUMBER BLANKS: one for each new person and for other members to fill out if they wish.

3. LEADER READS THE AAMAC PREAMBLE: Adults Anonymous Molested As Children is a society of men and women who share their experience, strength, and hope with each other in order to recover from having been molested as children. We have no dues or fees and are self-supporting through our own contributions. The only requirements for membership are an age of eighteen or more and a desire to recover from having been molested as a child. AAMAC is not allied with any sect, denomination, religion, political or outside organization. It neither endorses nor opposes any causes, and has no opinions on outside issues; hence the AAMAC name ought never be brought into public controversy.

4. LEADER READS: We do not wish to offend anyone, but our workshop is closed to all but AMACs and those questioning whether they are AMACS. All others please leave now.

5. LEADER READS: All AMACs and those questioning whether they are AMACs are welcome, regardless of their past. However, if you are an AMAC perpetrator and disclose that you have molested a child, but have not dealt with this matter through the proper authorities, we are bound both by moral obligation and by law to report you. We suggest that you deal with that problem first and not place the burden of your disclosure upon us. This reponsibility will allow us all to participate freely and not have any secrets. In AAMAC, we are concerned with the effects of having been molested as children upon our adult lives. Otherwise, the identity of our members and everything we say here is strictly confidential.

6. LEADER CHOOSES SOMEONE TO READ THE AAMAC TWELVE STEPS.

7. LEADER CHOOSES SOMEONE TO READ THE AAMAC TWELVE TRADITIONS.

8. LEADER READS: Though we encourage everyone to participate in our workshops, do not feel obligated to share deeply personal and sensitive information about yourself with the group. Share only those things that you want to share. We need to feel comfortable and not be intimidated by attending these workshops. In accordance with the traditional anonymous program format, we ask that there be no crosstalk while the workshop is in session. If you have questions, write them down and we will be happy to answer them to the best of our ability after the workshop has ended.

9. LEADER READS: Let's have a ten-minute coffee break.

10. LEADER OPENS WORKSHOP FOR PARTICIPATION.

11. LEADER STOPS WORKSHOP TEN MINUTES BEFORE CLOSING TIME AND READS: It is time to close our workshop by passing the collection basket. We have no dues or fees and are self-supporting through our own contributions. Are there any announcements?

12. LEADER READS: We meet here every week at the same time. Thank you for being here. We hope to see you again next week. After the workshop, for those who care to join us, we meet at _____. We close our workshops with a moment of silent meditation for AMACs who still suffer, and for all who suffer from child abuse. Those who care to, please stand and join hands in our moment of silence.

AAMAC QUESTION-AND-ANSWER WORKSHOP

The Secretary chooses a Leader for this two-hour workshop.

The Question-and-Answer Workshop should be heavily supported by long-time members of AAMAC. This type of workshop gives everyone an opportunity to interact with other AMACs and AAMAC as a whole. It is a great tool that can be utilized in many ways to set the new AAMAC member on the road to recovery. The Secretary should save all questions from the basket and use them again during a slow meeting when they run out of new questions. Also, from time to time, the Secretary can send the questions to AAMAC WSO, Inc. for possible inclusion in the AAMAC literature. These questions provide insight for our literature and will help us develop better ways to reach AMACs who still suffer.

This is a very simple workshop to conduct. Use the General Format for all AAMAC workshops. Along with that, provide the workshop participants with pencils and paper. Instruct them to write some questions, not to sign their names, and to put the questions into the "Ask It" basket. The Leader then mixes up the questions and passes the basket around the table for each participant to draw a question. Then the Leader calls on participants to answer the questions they have drawn. A person who does not want to participate may at least read the question, so that others may respond. Always ask whether others want to add anything before going on to the next question.

AAMAC BOOKSTUDY/ PARTICIPATION WORKSHOP

The Secretary chooses a Leader for this two-hour workshop.

The Leader gives a short five- or ten-minute talk about her personal experience as an AMAC. Then the Leader calls on people to read a paragraph or two from our book, ADULTS ANONYMOUS MOLESTED AS CHILDREN. In this workshop we read the entire book, except the section, "Group Information and Guidelines." (Should the group wish to, they may also include this section in the readings.) The purpose of this workshop is to enhance discussion and interaction among those attending the workshop. Hurrying to complete reading a certain number of pages is not advised. After each paragraph or two, stop and ask for any comments. If the workshop wants to discuss a particular subject in-depth, let it happen. Chances are that the subject needs discussing. Don't try to go through the book in one session, completing entire chapters or a prearranged number of pages. Simply note where the workshop left off and continue from that point at the next Bookstudy Workshop.

This workshop has proven to be the most fertile so far as participation and content are concerned. Great healing occurs through this type of cooperative work.

AAMAC TWELVE STEP WORKSHOP

The Secretary chooses a Leader for this two-hour workshop.

The AAMAC Twelve Step study concept is simple. The workshop members start with Step One and share experiences and problems working that Step, or, if they have not yet worked it, what they think about it. The Leader reads the particular Step being discussed. At each Step study thereafter, the workshop discusses the next Step. If participation is lacking, then choose a general topic relating to AMACism and discuss that instead.

AAMAC ROTATING WORKSHOP

The Rotating Workshop consists of a different type workshop each week of the month. In months with five weeks, the group decides what the fifth week workshop will be. Use the formats for details of each specific workshop.

First Monday: Question-and-Answer Workshop
Second Monday: Bookstudy/Participation Workshop
Third Monday: Twelve Step Study Workshop
Fourth Monday: AAMAC Topic Discussion Workshop
Fifth Monday: Workshop votes on type of meeting
Then the cycle begins again and continues indefinitely.

These are only examples. You may wish to schedule differently, rather than using all four workshops in your plan. The combinations can be mixed up however the group chooses. We advise using the formats already provided for each workshop, but that is also optional. The Twelve Steps and Twelve Traditions should be read aloud in every AAMAC workshop. Always read the disclosure clause to warn participants that we are bound to report perpetrators. This precaution keeps our agenda open and on the table and maintains our integrity as an anonymous program for helping rather than for enforcement.

AAMAC FIVE LEGACIES

1. Discovery
2. Truth
3. Recovery
4. Unity
5. Service

COORDINATION OF LEGACIES WITH AAMAC STEPS AND TRADITIONS:

LEGACY   STEP   TRADITION

LEGACY	STEP	TRADITION
Discovery	1-4, 8, 10, 11	3, 5, 10
Truth	1, 4, 5, 8, 10, 12	2, 3, 5-7, 11, 12
Recovery	1-12	1-12
Unity	2, 3, 5, 10, 12	1-12
Service	10-12	1-12

AAMAC FIVE LEGACIES OF RECOVERY AND SERVICE (LONG FORM)

FIRST LEGACY: DISCOVERY

Most members of AAMAC feel that the key to solving any problem is first to admit that a problem exists. Then we must go on to discover how our problem works, how it affects us in the practical conduct of our lives.

There is still more to do after we have overcome denial enough to admit that we have problems. Discovery in itself, we have learned, sets certain effects and changes into motion. Our denial, coupled with intuitive knowledge of what we must do to reveal more about our problems, is the paradox of a negative truth: by denying the facts, we AMACs paradoxically admit those facts.

Denial is a natural attempt to avoid pain. We were once aware of the facts which we denied. As time passed, we forgot the reason for our denial. We are thus burdened with problems which simultaneously mask the causes of the problems and are symptoms of those causes. This condition of secrecy is bewildering, for we are as blind to the connections between cause and effect as any onlooker.

Discovery is the key to overcoming our problems, but fear of discovery obstructs the way. This fear is not only anxiety about others' learning the deepest secrets of our lives. More subtly and profoundly, we fear our own conscious knowledge of ourselves, for if we see ourselves as we really are, we must take responsibility for our adult lives.

All AMACs suffer from the fear of discovery throughout our lives. The three components of that fear of discovery are as follows:

1. Fear of what we will discover within ourselves. Our natural reaction is denial.
2. Fear that we will find these same traits in other people and see our reflections in them. Our natural reaction is denial.
3. Fear that other people will discover the worst about us (our innermost secrets) and ridicule or reject us. Our natural reaction is denial.

The only tool that we know of which can lead us safely through this initial discovery is expressed in the Second Legacy, Truth.

SECOND LEGACY: TRUTH

It never occurred to us AMACs that, if we told ourselves the truth about us, we could eventually rid ourselves of many long-term problems. Telling our truth provides us with further information about ourselves because others like us then share their truth with us. Doing so, we sort of fill in the blanks for each other. This communal discovery to truth is the phenomenal healing process in our AAMAC workshops.

Most of us find that the truth generally begins with admitting to ourselves that we were molested as children. Many people would rather admit to having been forcibly raped than say that they were molested. The idea of molestation involves some sort of sexually deviant practices, abhorrent to most people in American society, and that fact results in stigma. AMACs feel generally responsible for these acts, never realizing that it was the people who molested us who perpetrated the sexual acts, not we ourselves. As children, we were only their victims. We wanted acceptance and love, among other things. We didn't even know what sex was. Denial, a natural reaction to such stigma, is common among AMACs.

When we admit that we are adults who were molested in childhood, we identify ourselves and, at the same time, describe our overall problem. Placing ourselves among AMACs is a statement that our childhood traumas have affected our adult lives. We realize that our truth-seeking will never make us perfect. But if we can learn to be honest about our dishonesty, our imperfections, our tragic flaws, we can improve immeasurably. And whom do we trust with such confidential information? We share it with people who have experienced problems like our own. It is easier to reveal ourselves among one another than to hide the truth from ourselves and all the world. We hope that AMACs who are experiencing severe emotional problems will also seek psychotherapy from a qualified professional. In most cases, this support speeds and enhances an AMAC's recovery.

Our years of experience NOT doing the things we suggest here proved that such passivity led to perpetual complication of our own and our families' lives. Facing the facts of our past helps us to overcome our fear of discovery and denial and leads us into our Third Legacy, which is Recovery.

THIRD LEGACY: RECOVERY

The word "recovery" means different things to different people. We in AAMAC have our own interpretation of what recovery represents. One thing is certain: our recovery does not mean that we are cured! The closest we in AAMAC have been able to come to a definition is this: recovery is our acceptance of and surrender to the truth about us as individuals, and our growing comfort with our identity as adults who were molested in childhood.

We expect no fanfare or ticker tape parades during the course of our recovery. That is not to say that we don't appreciate some strokes and emotional support for our efforts. We just want to live reasonably comfortable lives, happy and free from the bondage of our past. Those haunting memories of our molestation have held us captive long enough. As we understand the concept, we have recovered when we no longer suffer extensively from our childhood traumas, and when we have learned to intervene in our own problems so as not to go on living in trouble we once knew as adults.

Our addiction to denial either loses its power or claims victory over us. We members of AAMAC agree that there is no painless way of life. Once we accept that fact, we have realized the essence of our recovery, having shattered illusion and embraced reality. The word "reality" means that we know, rather than imagine, what is going on with us and in our surroundings. We are then, for the most part, comfortable with ourselves. We have learned only too well that it is less painful to know something than to suspect something and fear what we may discover or to deny what plainly confronts us.

Along with our acceptance and surrender comes eventual humility, which allows us to serve other people. This heartfelt humility brings us the quality of tolerance not only toward ourselves but toward others as well, a quality vital to our service involving other AMACs. In order to reach this plane of recovery, to reach out, we must first become unified in wholenesss ourselves. We must then define what our service to others will entail and to whom we will give this service. Since we cannot give away what we do not have, it has been necessary for us first to serve ourselves in our own recovery. Our outreach, in turn, ensures our own recovery as we progress along the path.

From this point on, we are engaged in life as never before, and the Fourth Legacy, Unity, evolves. We are fortunate survivors. We are able to see more clearly, looking back at the trouble we once were in. Many AMACs never live to enjoy the hope we have found. Many never unburden themselves and return the past to its rightful owners. But now, in AAMAC, adults who have suffered all their lives from their childhood molestation can recover if they choose.

FOURTH LEGACY: UNITY

We AMACs come from all backgrounds and social classes. Our common bond is our shared experience of having been molested in childhood. Since we share common causes and effects, we are bonded, like a family, and naturally motivated to help one another toward recovery. This unity creates the most fertile ground for growing trust, open communication, and loving service to one another.

Somebody stole our childhood, and we are angry. But now we no longer stand alone, in isolation. We are unified in a single purpose, which relieves us of anger toward one another, with no need to strike out and attack in anticipated self-defense. We have all known pain enough.

Treasuring the principles that have brought us toward recovery, we have learned to stand up to people who try to undermine the procedures that are the protection and the strength of AAMAC workshops, our Twelve Traditions. We come to AAMAC to change ourselves, not AAMAC. The basic concepts of our society have been tried and proven to work. Nobody who comes to an AAMAC workshop leaves empty-handed. Controversy over the framework of our society certainly diverts us from our purpose; once diverted, we fall into disharmony and disunity. That is why love and tolerance is our code. For most of our lives, we were too self-centered in our own defense to be unified with anyone or anything for long. But now we have a program of our own to help us. Value it and protect it.

If we choose to grow, then we must experience our own pain and accept ownership of it. It is that very pain which instills in each of us true empathic understanding for each other. Unity is the result of remembering where we came from, how destructive our old ways were to ourselves and others. It brings us here for the new people entering our society and motivates us to preserve for them what has worked so well for ourselves.

Now at last we identify with a group of people. We can discuss with them a subject on which we are all experts. We know that, in order to keep what we have, we must give it away. Our only protection from slipping back into selfishness and self-centeredness is to give of ourselves. That goal becomes our Fifth Legacy, Service.

FIFTH LEGACY: SERVICE

Our Five Legacies embody the reasons AAMAC came into existence. The Fifth Legacy is the ultimate expression of our purpose: to help ourselves and others recover and to carry our AAMAC message to AMACs who still suffer. No group, regardless of its nature, can exist for long without reaching out to others. New people are the lifeblood of any program. If you find that your AAMAC workshop is deteriorating, chances are that it has deviated too far from the tried and proven path and abandoned mutual love. That destroys its unified identity and purpose. It is also probable that few new people are being brought into the fold. A healthy workshop expands until it reaches capacity (fifteen or twenty members) and then opens a meeting on another night. No AAMAC workshop can survive without love among the members and outreach to AMACs who still suffer.

Dissension is a ruthless destroyer. Let us always remember that we grew up aimlessly, becoming extremely self-centered in our chosen self-destructive ways of life. We cannot continue now to grow unless we look outside ourselves. Service is indispensable to our own betterment, for through it we gain insight and value which are attainable in no other way.

Obviously, we can help with the routine work, contribute money, and share the responsibility in the General Service structure. But we also fulfill our humane function of service when we support our AAMAC society and workshop; keep open minds, speaking well of each other; avoid open, angry confrontation; and refrain from pressuring or demanding personal disclosure from others.

Let us not forget the good that we do ourselves by serving others, attending AAMAC workshops regularly, and sharing our insights in recovery. Remember also the love and comfort given us by those who came before us and paved our way. Our generosity to others is a great medicine for healing whatever ails us. Whether we're making the coffee at the workshop, greeting a new member, exploring our own lives in formal discussion, or associating at a local coffee shop after a meeting—anything that carries the AAMAC message is an act of service. Our Fifth Legacy is a great beacon that lights the future. It is vital to our common survival.